"Welcome to Iran!"

CHRISTIAN ENCOUNTERS WITH SHIA MUSLIMS

Evelyn and Wallace Shellenberger

iUniverse LLC
Bloomington

CONTENTS

INTRODUCTION

We had been in Iran for two weeks. Our professor, with whom we were reading the Quran, stopped, became quiet, and then looked at us and said, "Islam is evangelistic, and some people here will want you to become Muslim. You may sense an affinity to Islam. But we want you here as Christians. We want to learn from you how Christians live, and if you think you might become Muslim, you must pack your suitcases and go home. Welcome to Iran!"

Within those first two weeks in Iran it became clear that a face-to-face dialogue is so important in a world of news bites and stereotypes. Human beings have a tendency to view those we do not know personally through the lens of the media. This tends to portray a partial and sometimes biased view of others. Stories and images of Iran common to media sources help form impressions of Iran and its people as "fanatics," part of the "axis of evil," "hostage holders," "haters of Israel," or "developers of nuclear weapons." Relationships between the United States and Iran have been strained since the Iranian Revolution in 1979—thus, tourists have not been able to travel freely to experience Iran for themselves.

The famous Persian poet Rumi wrote a remarkable story about an elephant in a dark room, which forms the foundation for the writing of this book:

An elephant in a dark house had been brought in for exhibition. Many people came to see it; each came into the darkness. Since seeing with the eye was not possible, in the darkness each rubbed it with a hand.

This one's palm felt the trunk and said, "It is like a pipe."

Another's hand touched its ear; "It moves like a fan."

The next rubbed a palm on its leg and said, "This elephant must be shaped like a pillar."

Another placed a hand on its back and said to himself, "This elephant is like a throne."

In this manner each touched a part and understood the elephant from that part.

From their varied points of contact each description differed: one felt a curve, another a straight line. If each had carried a candle, the exclusive differences in what they said would have mellowed.[1]

Where is the candle that will light up the dark room in order to reveal a less-biased view of Iran, a more "mellowed" understanding of this important country and its people?

In 2001, we had the opportunity to live among the Iranian people for three years as part of a student-exchange program sponsored by Mennonite Central Committee (MCC), a worldwide ministry of Anabaptist churches involved in relief, development, and peacebuilding efforts.

From 2004 to 2008 we led several North American–based learning tours to Iran in order to expand North American understandings and perspectives of Iran and the Iranian people—in order to encourage North Americans to see through the light of their own candles. We returned to live in Iran from 2008 to 2009 in an effort to help develop more opportunities for exchanges between the United States and Iran.

The student-exchange program was an important development, both for the Iranians and North Americans, since strained governmental relationships between the United States and Iran have not been conducive to such arrangements. So how did such a student-exchange program develop in the midst of these governmental tensions?

Mennonite Central Committee began its work in Iran following an earthquake in 1990. This earthquake devastated the Gilan and Zanjan Provinces of northeastern Iran. At that time a humanitarian partnership was forged between MCC and the Iranian Red Crescent

Society (IRCS), a partnership that continues today. The two organizations work together to provide relief to refugees, to aid in reconstruction efforts following earthquake disasters, to provide drought-relief efforts, and to organize health-related programs. This partnership between MCC and IRCS paved the way for the student-exchange program, which began in 1998.

The interest for a student-exchange program grew out of a similar program during the Cold War, when MCC sponsored a program in Eastern Europe where students studied in Warsaw, Belgrade, Prague, and East Berlin in an effort to make friends and build relationships with people living in Communist countries not easily accessible to people of Canada and the United States. These grassroots, people-to-people exchanges were important ways of working toward international peace and friendship among countries "at war" with each other.

The importance of student-exchange programs has been recognized by the US Department of State. "People-to-people exchanges are a vital component of our national security strategy and perhaps our most valuable public diplomacy asset. Many exchange participants report that they are forever changed by their direct involvement with the American people." Exchange programs create bridges that can be crossed in both directions.[2]

Based on the history of the important working relationships between the IRCS and MCC, an agreement was signed between MCC and the Imam Khomeini Education and Research Institute (IKERI) in Qom, Iran, for a student-exchange program. In this exchange two North American students would be hosted in Iran to study Islam, the Persian language, and Iranian history and culture, and two Iranian students would be hosted in North America to study religion, to interact with Christian communities and gain a deeper understanding of Western culture. The foundational goals of this program were to build relationships and friendships between the United States, Canada, and Iran and to learn about and engage in each country's respective faiths and religions in order to dismantle walls of misunderstanding, suspicion, ignorance, and intolerance erected over the years.

Directors of the student-exchange program with the Shellenbergers.

The chapters in this book are based on our experience as students in this exchange program. They grew out of our personal engagements and studies, and they portray aspects of Iran we were able to see with the lights of our candles—the "eye of our hearts."

Most of the writing is in the form of stories and poetry, and it is our intention to focus on the positive aspects of our experience in Iran. Storytelling has been part of the human experience since time immemorial, and we believe we can enter another's life more fully through story. Poetry also easily crosses boundaries. The Persian poets speak from the heart, a language that more easily engages the other.

Chapter 1 begins the story of our life in Iran as we cross the boundaries into Iran and settle into a life and culture very different from our own. This chapter's title, "Sweet Lemons—Life in Iran," employs a sweet lemon as a metaphor for how we paradoxically experienced life in Iran.

Chapter 2, "Tea, Fruit, and Gifts—Hospitality," describes the fruitful hospitality of the Iranian people—hospitality experienced in some very surprising places. It was in Iran that we experienced being truly welcomed as a stranger in a foreign land.

Chapter 3, "Shared Heart, Shared Humanity," reveals the Iranian conviction that unless one can share in the pain of others, one cannot be called a human.

In chapter 4, "Persian Carpets—Weavers of Dialogue," we share our experience of the Iranians as active, contributing partners in dialogue—be it the ongoing dialogue of life, religious matters, controversial issues, or more structured theological discussions.

Perhaps the most surprising aspect of Iran for the American people is its commitment to peace and justice. In chapter 5, "Nightingales and Feather Dusters—Iranian Peacemakers," we see a people deeply concerned for peace and justice and insulted when linked to the term "terrorist."

As we spoke more than 350 times to people in North America about our experience in Iran, in nearly every session we were asked to talk about the status of women. In chapter 6, "Covered Heads—Uncovered Stereotypes," the light of our candle exposes some unexpected surprises.

The Iranians have given the world poetry that awakens the heart and challenges the way we live and how we see things. In chapter 7, "Gifts of Poetry," one can read some of this remarkable poetry (translated by coauthor Wally with the help of many Iranian friends).

The book ends with a chapter focusing on transformation, "Transformation—Seeing with the Eye of the Heart." As you will read in this chapter, even a ninety-seven-year-old woman can choose to view Islam and Iran in a new way when she is able to see Iran through stories and encounters never before heard or experienced.

In Iran there is a common saying: "When the heart does not see, hearing through the ears is of no use." May you be able to read this book with the eye of your heart.

—Wallace and Evelyn Shellenberger, February 2013

CHAPTER 1

Sweet Lemons—Life in Iran

Among the many delicious fruits in Iran, the most surprising is the sweet lemon—a fruit that looks like a lemon but tastes deceptively sweet, like a mild orange—a fruit that symbolizes the many surprises, paradoxes, or complexities of life in Iran as we experienced it.

A few of these paradoxes include a seven-thousand-year-old culture and architecture existing with modern-day skyscrapers and traffic; turban-clad Islamic clerics with cell phones in hand; chador-clad women with active professional involvement; designer jeans and shoes underneath coats and chadors; tissue boxes in homes and offices with cultural taboos about blowing one's nose in public; a dislike of Western culture but enjoyment of American movies, cartoons, music, and toys; hesitancy to engage in political dialogue with eagerness to engage in conversations about faith, education, and culture; Superman, Batman, and princesses in Iranian stores together with Islamic children's books and toys; high regard for the Iranian educational system with many youth studying abroad or dreaming of studying abroad; frequent statements of love for the American *people* with statements against the American *government*; and two Americans (us!) warmly welcomed to study in the conservative Islamic city of Qom, a city that houses few other American personnel or interests.

Evelyn and Wallace Shellenberger

Making the Decision to Live in Iran

Our journey to Iran began in 1969, after we had completed four years of medical work in Nigeria, West Africa, during the Biafran Civil War. The experience of living in Nigeria grew in us a deep appreciation for other cultures, history, and people groups, and when we left Nigeria in 1969, we decided we would engage once again in cross-cultural service when our children were grown and able to live on their own. The opportunity to do this came in 2001, when we received a phone call from the director of human resources at the MCC headquarters in Akron, Pennsylvania.

We had been applying to various service organizations, volunteering our gifts to be used where needed, and had begun to learn Spanish, assuming we would be going to a Spanish-speaking country. In fact, we were working our way through the Rosetta Stone Spanish program when the phone call from MCC rang a different opportunity.

The human resources person on the other end asked if we would consider an assignment in the student-exchange program developed just a few years earlier in Iran. As we learned about this program, we became deeply drawn to the possibility of living among the Iranian Muslims, building friendships and relationships, partnering in dialogue, and learning about the traditions and faiths of others. After much thought and discernment, we signed a three-year commitment to participate with MCC in this student-exchange program to live and learn in Iran.

Preparing to Cross the Boundaries

We were not unaware of the various challenges we would face in this journey to Iran. Obtaining student visas and learning the Persian language and customs were two such challenges.

The challenge of obtaining student visas to Iran led us to discover new places as we waited for our very first student visas to be approved by the Iranian government. While we waited, we flew to the Philippine Islands for a week of meetings, expecting to pick up our visas at the Iranian embassy that same week. After arriving in Manila we discovered the visas were not yet ready, which enabled us to enjoy three weeks discovering a new country and its culture, continue our language study, and anxiously wait. That day finally arrived and the excitement was memorable as our eyes were glued to our passports and we watched that yellow student visa being stamped into the empty, waiting page.

For the language-learning part, we studied with an Iranian student at Indiana University, spent two weeks at the Boston Language Institute in intensive-language immersion, and purchased a Persian language program and various books to study.

Learning the Persian language was difficult, and our age—we were in our sixties at the time—did nothing to help us. The alphabet, similar to Arabic, was unrecognizable, and reading and writing from right to left was awkward. Our mouths and tongues struggled to pronounce the harsh *kh* sound found in so many Persian words, and the absence of vowels in the written script meant that our ears had to be trained to hear the various vowel sounds. However, dialogue with a diversity of Iranians and reading Persian poetry became possible only because of this language training. When we finally arrived in Iran, we felt accomplished to be able to speak and write a few basic sentences in Persian.

In addition to language training, we spent time learning about Iranian culture and customs to prepare for our journey to Iran. For this learning, it was important to spend time with our Iranian counterparts in the student-exchange program, two Iranian families living in Toronto. When we visited these families in Toronto, we were warmly welcomed by fragrant Persian foods and hospitality. In addition, one of the women, Masumeh, helped me (Evie) prepare for life as a woman in Iran—a life that included proper dress and custom.

Masumeh took me to her bedroom, pulled out several scarves, and carefully taught me how to put on the scarf so that none of my hair would show. The scarves were beautiful and colorful, and as I tried on each one, Masumeh would comment whether it was folded right or came far enough down my forehead.

She also introduced me to the *chador* and *mantow* I would wear to cover my body. The chador is literally translated as *tent* in Persian. It is approximately nine yards of fabric, usually black, that covers the body but leaves the face and hands exposed. The mantow is a long, tunic-style coat. She informed me that only my face and hands should show when out in public. She pulled several lightweight coats from her closet and had me try them on. When she noticed they were too long and too wide, she quickly pulled out her sewing machine, sat on the floor, and adjusted the length and width.

How pleased she looked when I modeled the coat and scarf for her. I laughed to see myself in such attire and asked her to take a picture so I could show my friends and family how I would dress in Iran. Throughout the "modeling" session we were laughing together, and I knew then that I would enjoy the company of Iranian women!

Before leaving the room, Masumeh packed several scarves and coats for me to take to Iran. She also reminded me not to shake hands with men unless they first offered their hand, and she encouraged me to buy shoes that could be removed easily before entering homes, mosques, or office settings, as is the custom in Iran. Later in the evening, her preschool son taught me the Persian names for colors, and by the end of the evening, I had learned a few things about the new life ahead of me in Iran.

Another important encounter we had before leaving was to meet the Iranian ambassador to the United Nations, and I was instructed to dress in a scarf and coat. I found my stomach tight and body tense as we entered his office waiting room: What would I say? What would he ask? Where would I sit? Would I remember not to offer my hand for a handshake? The point of our visit was to inform the ambassador of our decision to go to Iran and to explain how we saw our assignment there. Needless to say, I was looking forward to this visit being over.

When the ambassador opened the door to call us into his office, it seemed this visit may not be so difficult. He was laughing and immediately offered us tea, fruit, and candy. He talked about Iran and his enthusiasm about such an exchange program. We similarly expressed our enthusiasm about the opportunity. He quoted Persian poets, and we noticed Persian poetry books on the table and Persian paintings on his wall.

As we were leaving, he reminded us of the importance of Jesus to the Iranians and blessed us, saying, "Go and shine like Jesus!"

Perhaps the primary challenge in crossing the boundaries and barriers to live in Iran was *attitude*. How did we prepare and see ourselves as students, learners, and guests in Iran? What stereotypes and prejudices did we need to let go of to be open to what awaited us?

The most helpful advice came from an American Muslim living in Iran. He reminded us that in preparing to go, we would need to pack a variety of things, but the most important, he said, are smiling faces, faith, hope, love, open minds, sincerity, questions, criticism, doubts, respect, appreciation, wonder, patience, forgiveness, sensitivity, piety, fear of God, honor, honesty, alertness, awareness, two books, and some coffee. Important advice! He suggested we think of this experience as a sort of pilgrimage or visitation to a holy site, knowing that a pilgrimage is taken for the sake of God, and for experiencing and encountering God.

With these words we left the United States and began our pilgrimage. A one-day stay in Dubai was our last stop before heading for Iran.

✸

We left Dubai early one June morning in 2001 to make the final flight to Iran. The emotions of this flight were mixed and contradictory: excitement/fear, questioning/anticipation, anxiety/peace, doubts/hope. We couldn't eat the lovely breakfast that was served to us; the knots in our stomachs took up too much room.

The airliner began its descent into Tehran. We looked out the windows to see a huge, modern-looking city, snow-covered mountains, and much pollution. As the plane descended, women began grabbing carry-on luggage and searching for scarves to cover their heads. The stewardess announced that all women must cover their heads before entering the airport. I reached for my scarf and tried to remember all the steps necessary to wear it properly. Excitement on the plane was palpable as many Iranians looked forward to reuniting with family.

The next hurdle was moving through the immigration process, where our visas were validated without difficulty. As we passed the airport security area, we saw families with bouquets of flowers waiting for their loved ones. We were welcomed by a professor, who wore a brown robe and a white turban, from the institute where we would be studying. Because we had met him once earlier, he immediately recognized us in the crowd of passengers, came over to meet us in the security area, and managed to get us through customs with a nod of his head. Nothing was checked; no questions were asked. We walked with him through the crowded airport to a waiting car and driver who would take us to our new home in Qom.

From Tehran to Qom

Since we had read so extensively about Tehran and Qom before our journey to Iran, we were eager to finally experience these places firsthand. Reading about the crowded streets in Tehran, for example, was one thing, but experiencing the mass of cars, motorcycles, and people was quite another.

Families on motorcycles weaved in and out of traffic; cars and taxis moved quickly, also weaving in and out of traffic; a couple of taxis even drove *against* traffic. Meanwhile, a car was honking and trying to back up in the moving traffic, while pedestrians seemed to be crossing the crowded streets with apparent ease. (Incidentally, when we led learning tours to Iran years later, we noticed that one of the favorite activities among the participants was to stand on a corner in Tehran and watch the traffic.)

We were amazed at how clean (excluding the pollution) and modern the city appeared. The outside of many buildings were painted with pictures of martyrs from the Iran-Iraq War. Pictures of Imam Khomeini, leader of the 1979 Iranian Revolution, and the current Supreme Leader, Ayatollah Khamenei, were visible nearly everywhere. Many small stores with all sorts of merchandise lined the boulevards, and shoppers seemed to enjoy looking in the store windows. The one word that describes Tehran on first impression: *crowded.*

A street in the modern city of Tehran depicting pictures of Imam Khomeini, Supreme Leader Ayatollah Khamenei, and martyrs of the Iran-Iraq War.

I was eager to see how the Iranian women were dressed and noticed a wide variety of *hijab*—the Muslim dress code for properly covering the body. Many women were wearing the traditional chador, but some wore tunic-style coats over designer jeans and scarves that fell back on the head. I had been told that my head should be completely covered, so it was perplexing to see so many women with so much of their hair showing. I wondered what would be expected of me.

Iranian women wearing a variety of hijab.

After leaving the city, we drove on a modern four-lane highway that would take us to Qom, our final destination. The landscape between Tehran and Qom is mostly barren and desert-like. One attraction along the way is the holy shrine of Imam Khomeini—a shrine that millions of people visit each year to remember the imam, to pray, and to give alms. Our host was excited to point out this shrine as we traveled by it. Later during our stay we would visit the shrine ourselves.

As we finally entered the city of Qom, a large, empty, and silent Ferris wheel loomed in front of us—an odd welcome for the most holy city in Iran. We were expecting to see a beautiful mosque; instead, we were greeted by this silent Ferris wheel—an enigma that prepared us for the many other enigmas and paradoxes we would experience while living in Iran.

Our First Taste of Iran

It was lunchtime when we arrived in Qom. Our driver took us to the home of one of the professors at the institute where we would be studying. He, his wife, and their preschool son warmly welcomed us into their home, where lunch was waiting.

We were struck by the beautiful Persian carpets lining the floors, the red pillows lining the walls of the living room, and most importantly, the smiles and gestures of welcoming faces. We were instructed to sit on the carpets where we were served *chai* ("hot tea") and fruit. The watermelon, peaches, cherries, and cucumbers tasted refreshing on this 110-degree summer day. We were a bit worried one of us might spill tea on the beautiful carpets, but this worry soon vanished when the preschool son was also served tea on the carpet.

It was here that we first learned the proper way of drinking tea in Iran, which is to put a sugar cube in your mouth and hold it on your tongue while you drink. I (Evie) somehow never learned to do this and instead would drop the cube into my cup and experience the sweetness of the tea with the last swallow.

As we finished the tea and fruit, our hostess collected the cups and plates and then spread a plastic tablecloth, which she called a *sofreh*, on the floor. Her husband and son helped set the sofreh with plates, silverware, glasses, and a box of tissues, which are used as napkins in Iran. A stereotype of ours was shaken as we watched the men of the household set the sofreh and participate in the preparation and serving of the meal. Where did we get the impression that it was the duty of women in Iran to serve men? This was one of many stereotypes that would be challenged during our time in Iran.

A typical Iranian sofreh, neatly arranged on a fine Persian carpet.

Then a beautiful platter of saffron rice, colorfully decorated with red berries and pieces of pistachio nuts, was gently placed on the waiting sofreh, followed by *khoresh* (Persian for "stew"), an Iranian stew consisting of some combination of lamb, red kidney beans, and many herbs and spices all simmered together for hours.

The last dish to arrive was a lettuce salad with a dressing resembling Thousand Island; salads are customarily eaten at the end of the meal.

This was our first Persian meal and one that was to be repeated many times during our stay in Iran. Simply delicious!

Our New Home

We were eager to see where we would be living the next few years and had been told we would find it comfortable and modern. It was more than we expected! An apartment on the second level of an Iranian home had been rented for us. Our landlord, an owner of a small grocery store, lived in the apartment on the ground level with his wife and five children. They eagerly greeted us when we arrived, and though they spoke no English, we sensed they were excited to have us living with them. The children later became our teachers as they helped us learn Iranian customs and practices.

We took off our shoes as we entered the building and with anticipation climbed the stairs leading to our new home. With a quick glance we knew we would have everything we needed: a fully equipped kitchen; a large living area with a table, sofa, and chairs; a large bedroom with a queen-size bed; a water cooler to help cool the hot, dry air; a bathroom with a shower; and a Western-style toilet. And then there were the luxuries: a TV and DVD player; computers; mirrors; a deck opening into the courtyard; fresh fruit and pastries waiting for us on the table; and a large electric samovar (a metal container holding hot water for making tea). In our bedroom we found special mirrors on the dresser and two candle stands, traditionally given as wedding gifts. As we looked around our new home, we appreciated seeing the traditions of both cultures—Iran and the US—represented in our furnishings.

Discovering the City of Qom

During our first week in Qom we were eager to get out into the streets and experience the city that would be our home for the next three years. The first afternoon we arrived we walked around the streets and were amazed at how quiet they were, with very few people walking around. It didn't take long for us to realize that the afternoon temperature of 110 was the reason we saw so few people and the reason most of the shops were closed: it was too hot to be out and about at this time of day.

The scene, however, was completely shifted later in the evening as the streets and shops were full of people. The environment seemed very different from Tehran. Most women were clothed in the traditional chador; Muslim clerics in traditional robes and turbans were everywhere. Many tourists, coming in buses from various cities and towns throughout Iran, were gathered around the burial place of Fatemeh, sister to one of the important imams in Shia Islam, Imam Reza. Hazrat-e-Masumeh (Fatemeh) died on her way to visit her brother in the ninth century CE and was buried in Qom. Her shrine makes Qom known as the second-holiest city in Iran, second only to Mashhad, where her brother, Imam Reza, is buried. Many tourists bring tents and camp on the ground just outside the shrine.

As we walked around the area of the shrine, we were amazed at the many bookstores lining the boulevard. We met students of many different nationalities who had come to Qom to study more about Shia Islam. In addition, the Arabic open market was nearby, and if you could make it through the crowds and motorcycles that filled the walkways, you could find a variety of spices, nuts, dried fruits, fresh fruits, fresh vegetables, fish, lamb, and beef.

Of the many diverse people we observed as we walked around the city, we saw no homeless people and very few beggars. What we did see on nearly every block, however, were blue boxes resembling parking meters set up to collect money for the poor. We frequently saw Iranians drop coins into these boxes. The acts of care and generosity reminded us that the poor and the hungry exist in all lands and places and all of us are responsible to offer our care and support.

Other than the people, the things we enjoyed most in Qom were the abundance of fresh produce. Stands were situated on nearly every block, and fresh fruits and vegetables—pomegranates, sweet lemons, blood oranges, cherries, melons, peaches, pears, apples, persimmons, grapes, and sweet cucumbers and eggplant—could be purchased every day. We found joy in cooking and eating fresh foods, and we were thrilled to carry out our "trash" each week—a small plastic bag filled mainly with peelings.

One of many collection boxes located throughout Iran.

And the bread! Just a block from our apartment was a typical Iranian bakery where we could buy hot bread each day. It's baked on heated stones in a large oven. Once you wait in line and buy your bread—a big, flat loaf—you then lay it on a rack to be sure all the stones are sorted out. This bread is the primary breakfast food in Iran and is usually spread with butter, soft cheese, whipped cream, walnuts, jam, or honey. Served with hot tea it is delicious!

The cleanliness of the city was quite surprising. Each evening we saw men sweeping away the trash that had accumulated. Recycling seemed not to be a concern, except for bread. It was a common sight to see young boys pushing a cart through the streets collecting stale bread to feed animals. We were told, "Bread is sacred" and should not be wasted.

As we traveled through Iran, many Iranians would ask us why we lived in Qom. They would remark how hot it is in Qom, how salty the water tastes, how conservative the women dress, and how it offers no "entertainment." One of our many hosts shared the expression, "If you live in Qom during the summer, it is because you either have no 'cents' or no 'sense.'"

Indeed, the weather was terribly hot in the summer, the water salty, and the conservative atmosphere of the city palpable. However, the hospitality, welcome, and warmth of the people we lived among trumped the more difficult parts.

Daily Life in Qom

The sound of *azan* calling Muslims to prayer woke us each morning. The rhythm of each day consisted primarily of going to classes and studying. We would walk about twenty minutes to meet with our professors, who were prepared to help us with our learning. All our professors were fluent in English, and most held a PhD.

Our first task was to continue learning the Persian language in order to read, write, and speak it. As we began our study, a language teacher would come to our apartment for four hours and instruct us. He was not an English speaker, so it was a challenge for us to communicate.

As we walked to other classes, children on the street also functioned as our "teachers." They recognized that we were foreigners and would greet us and try out the few English words they knew: "Good morning," "What time is it?," and "What is your name?" We would answer in Persian and they would run away giggling.

On one particular day when we were walking where the children usually met us, we noticed some chalk writing on the sidewalk that read, "We love you." As we paused to look at the message, we heard children laughing. We were delighted to be on the receiving end of such a "love letter" written for us by Iranian children in our own native language.

The Iranians were delighted to hear us try to speak their language, in spite of our many mistakes. On one occasion we were presenting some chocolates to a group of professors, thanking them for their time, all the while speaking in Persian. This was followed by loud clapping. Then, the professor who'd received our gift remarked that they would enjoy the sweet chocolates. "But even sweeter," he said, "is to hear Persian spoken by foreign tongues."

Foundational to our formal studies was an in-depth study of the Quran—the Islamic holy book. Previous to our arrival in Iran we had never read the Quran, and like most Americans, knew very little about it. Under the guidance of a gentle, knowledgeable professor we spent a year reading and studying the Quran together, chapter by chapter, verse by verse. This professor also knew the Bible well and invited questions and responses to both sacred texts.

Our three years of study included classes in Islamic beliefs and practices; Islam and the family; peace and Islam; Islamic spirituality; Shia Islam; Iranian history; Islamic jurisprudence; and the poetry of Hafez. These were the formal learning experiences that helped us gain new perspectives of our own Christian faith and new understandings about Islam.

Some of the teachings we have appreciated about Islam are summarized below. The recognition and understanding of the rich inner aspect, or more mystical dimension, of Islam became a significant aspect of our interfaith dialogue.

1. The primary emphasis in Islam on the *compassion and benevolence of God* is noteworthy. This is repeated more than sixty times each day in the course of a Muslim's daily prayer and is a central theme in the Quran.

2. The importance of knowing God comes not only through revelation but from the signs of God in the natural world and through knowing oneself.

3. The heart is like a mirror that reflects the attributes of God. It is important to remove our personal attachments for the things of this world, which act as dirt on the mirror of our

heart, resulting in a blurred image of God reflected to others and ourselves.

4. The positive nature of the human being is emphasized, which, when not impeded by excessive attachments to worldly matters, can, with the help of revelation, achieve perfection and nearness to God.

5. The continuous praise of God is important: praise for who God *is* rather than what God *does* for us.

6. As we seek to know God, we must realize that we are the creature seeking to know our creator. In this state of humility we recognize that our desire to know God is best understood as God's desire in us to seek God.

7. One must strive to be in a constant state of prayer. A word or phrase that one knows well and repeats often can become a part of self and therefore nearly always in one's mind or on one's tongue.

8. Extending peace and safety to others is a daily act. This is shown by the use of many words that have, as their root, "selm." The most common usage would be *salam*, the greeting given when meeting another. This is a way of ensuring that the one being greeted is safe from any harm from the greeter.

9. Faith finds many verbal expressions in daily life, such as *salam* ("peace"), *enshalla* ("if God wills"), and *khoda hafez* ("may God protect you"). At the beginning of any activity, the phrase "In the name of God, the merciful, the compassionate" is used. These expressions are used dozens of times a day in the course of ordinary interaction with others.

10. Islam, particularly Shia Islam, gives great importance to justice. Justice is known as one of the characteristics of Shia Islam.

11. Individual human rights are seen in the context of community. Rights are commonly expressed as the right of another over "me," or in other words, my duty toward another.

12. Freedom has value—not as individual freedom to do what I want but freedom to choose to follow the way to God, freedom to choose to achieve perfection, and freedom to choose to submit to a community.

13. Pious actions are approved of by God only when there is an intention to please God. They are of no value, in terms of one's salvation, if the intention is to please others.

14. There is an emphasis on following God's way only and not deviating from this "straight path" by following the ways of the world.

15. Much effort is placed on the education and support of the young and adults in being faithful to God's way.

16. Islam maintains a close association with the faith of the prophets we know as the great personalities of the Old Testament. In Christianity there tends to be some dissociation with the faith of the Old Testament saints along with a higher emphasis on the New Testament and Jesus.

17. Dialogue between faiths is more related to actions and behavior than words. The fruits of the spirit, as Christians know them in Galatians and Colossians, are important to keep in mind when meeting with persons of another faith.

18. The teachings of Jesus and his followers for the first three hundred years had nothing to do with war. Islam accepts war as a part of living on this earth and gives rules for the conduct of war. Jesus prohibits it and Islam regulates it.

19. The word *jihad* literally means to struggle or to strive or to put forth great effort. It refers to the struggle of the soul to overcome all the obstacles that would keep one from God.

20. Mary, the mother of Jesus, is greatly revered and honored in the Quran and in the daily life of Muslims. Many girls are named after her, and many have reported that Mary is one important woman they would look up to as a model of faith.

21. Original sin is not part of Islamic beliefs. It is acknowledged that Adam and Eve did disobey God, but they were forgiven.

In addition to our learning at the institute, informal learning experiences occurred daily in the marketplace, in homes, while traveling, and in restaurants, universities, tourist sites, and almost everyplace we visited. One day when we were sitting in a teahouse in the mountains, a gathering of older men sat together drinking tea and telling stories. They invited us to join them at the table and began sharing stories about how life in Iran was different when they were young. Another time when we entered an art shop in Esfahan, the owner took out a paintbrush and instructed us on the art of the miniature paintings so popular in Iranian culture. And yet another time, as we sat in a restaurant in Shiraz, a student instructed us on how to smoke the water pipe.

A caring neighbor provided helpful hints for me as I struggled to learn how to use a squat toilet, and many a hostess took me into the kitchen to teach me how to use saffron and make Iranian rice. In addition, a young boy once told me how to recognize a friend when lost in a crowd of chador-clad women. He said, "Look at their shoes."

The Shellenbergers learning to smoke an Iranian water pipe.

We learned some beautiful phrases that Iranians use commonly. For example, it is considered impolite to have your back turned toward another, and when that happens, one asks to be excused. A common Iranian response is, "A rose has no back." When remarking about something being beautiful, the reply is often, "Your eyes see beauty." As we presented small gifts to those who invited us to a meal, a frequent response was, "Thank you. Your presence is a gift."

As much as we learned through formal and informal "training" in Iran, there were things we didn't learn very well, such as how to sit cross-legged on the floor for more than a hour while eating and visiting; how to hold my chador closed with my hands while carrying two bags of groceries and trying to get on a bus; how to keep my husband from stepping on my chador as we walked together; and how to wait until nine p.m. to finally eat dinner. In Iran, one way of showing honor to another is to offer, when walking through a door, that the other goes through the door first, saying, *befarmaid*— "you go first." It was not uncommon to be in a situation where one would offer, "Befarmaid," and the other would respond, *"Na, shoma befarmaid"* ("No, you go first"), and then the other would respond again, "Befarmaid," etc. This could continue for a long time. We wondered how many times befarmaid must be spoken before it was proper to go ahead and walk through the door.

Our daily life in Qom was full of many new things to learn and experience. As we left our apartment each day and walked into the street, we wondered what was waiting to be discovered and said a prayer that our minds, hearts, and eyes would always be open to what the day would bring.

Life beyond Qom

We had the opportunity to travel freely throughout all of Iran and see firsthand ancient cities, masterful works of art, beautiful mosques, Persian gardens in full bloom, palaces, Persian carpets boasting 350 knots per square inch, museums with ancient artifacts, bazaars extending for miles full of spices and Iranian crafts, churches, Jewish synagogues, shrines of famous Persian poets, and beautiful bridges and architectural structures. To experience the history and beauty of the country is unforgettable, but the greatest joy was meeting the diverse people throughout the country who warmly shared their lives, stories, and thoughts with us.

During our stay in Iran we received a letter from a friend who asked, "What does it feel like to live in an 'axis of evil' country?" We were surprised by such a question and wondered how we might respond. As I thought about it, I decided to respond by writing this friend about the day I had just experienced in this "axis of evil":

> I spent some time alone today shopping in some of the little stores in the bazaar. When I finished it was dark and the sky filled with stars. I decided to walk home to enjoy the night sky, and I felt safe walking here alone at night; I have no fear. I never felt safe walking alone at night in our southern Indiana

community. What does this say about how it is to live in an "axis of evil" country?

Later that night an Iranian couple, Muhammad and Mahnaz, who had studied in England, visited us and expressed their desire to promote dialogue between Christians and Muslims. Mahnaz had spent time in Catholic and Protestant communities learning more about Christianity. She had written a book titled *Love in Christianity and Islam*. She gave us a copy as a gift. We opened it and read: "This book is dedicated to the blessed memory of two of the greatest teachers and examples of ethical values throughout the history of humankind: Jesus and Muhammad." On the outside cover we read, "The seedbed of hatred is ignorance of the other; the seedbed of love is knowledge of the other." I hope this summary of my day will answer your question of what it is like to live in a country in the "axis of evil."

As we traveled throughout Iran during our three-year stay, we tried to write some of the reoccurring themes we heard as we entered conversation with others. Perhaps the following excerpts from the Iranians we met in our travels will provide a glimpse of the "other" and help dismantle a few bricks from the walls of misunderstandings.

"Feel at home here; it belongs to your God."—religious cleric

"You Americans have a right to have fear, but not phobia. That is a product of the media."—Islamic professor

"The world is like an ocean: poison spread in one part affects the others."—Islamic professor

"Who can forget that America created Saddam or bin Laden?"—Islamic professor

"Integrating church and state has meant the sacrifice of religion in Iran. Our youth are becoming less religious."—sociology professor

"Shia Muslims do not believe in terrorism or massacres. We don't kill innocent people."—Islamic professor

"Iranians want respect as a people with a valuable religious and cultural tradition."—Islamic professor

"Problems in a foreign culture stick out obviously to guests (e.g., inferior treatment of women), but we are used to the problems in our own society (e.g., sexual exploitation of women in advertising)."—American woman

"Where are you from? Welcome to Iran! We love Americans." —elderly Iranian man

"Please be our ambassadors and tell them we are not terrorists."—tour guide in Esfahan

"We must dialogue between cultures, nations, and civilizations. Centuries of history have shown us that this is the best way. We need each other. We are unable to alone meet the problems our world faces."—government representative from the Organization for Culture and Relationships

"What is the basis of Islamic morality? To become a more perfect mirror of God."—Islamic professor and author

"Worshipping God and serving people go hand in hand."—Islamic professor

"It matters to the whole world how Christians and Muslims relate to each other. Better understanding and peaceful relations are essential for the well-being of the world at large."—Islamic cleric

"Talk to people about what you have seen in Iran. If people understood us better relations would develop. We have little hope that our government leaders will resolve the conflicts. We need people-to-people contacts, not politicians. We need to figure out how to look at the issues with each other's eyes."—Iranian professor

"Are you Muslim?" ("No.") "Welcome! There is one God, and you know right and wrong, and I hope to see you in God's place, paradise."—female Iranian student

CHAPTER 2

Tea, Fruit, and Gifts—Hospitality

If there is one characteristic of the Iranian people that trumps all others, it is hospitality. The gift of welcome and hospitality was evident everywhere we traveled in Iran and was offered by young and old alike. In the Bible, the Greek word for "hospitality" is *philoxenia*, literally "love" (*philo*) of "stranger" (*xenia*).

In the Christian tradition, offering love to strangers (being hospitable) is commanded in both the Old and New Testaments and is a recurring theme throughout the Bible. Our Western minds don't often associate hospitality with "love of stranger," and it was through our experience of being offered love as a stranger in a foreign country that transformed our understanding of hospitality.

As we walked familiar and unfamiliar streets in Iran and engaged in conversations with "strangers," we heard the same phrase repeated over and over again: "Welcome to our country." We even "heard" this welcome on the tomb of the great King Cyrus of Persia when we visited it: "Welcome, pilgrim, I have been expecting you. Before you lies Cyrus, king of Asia, king of the world. All that is left of him is dust. Do not envy me."

Perhaps the culture of welcome has extended back thousands of years in Persian history. However, hearing and receiving so many expressions of welcome from so many different people felt new to us, and we were painfully reminded how the lack of welcome to strangers in our own country must feel. The Iranians, we realized, had much to teach us about hospitality.

The tomb of King Cyrus, in the process of renovation.

Drinking tea and sharing plates filled with delicious fruits and sweet cucumbers were common experiences of hospitality in Iran (Iranians *always* find time to visit and drink tea together). In homes, the samovar is always on the stove, ready to serve family and guests. Tea is most often served in a small glass called an *estekan*.

Before we began classes each day at the institute, tea would be carried into the room for us to enjoy. The polite response when served tea in Iran was either "thank you" or the interesting Persian phrase, *daste shoma dard nakone* ("May your hands not pain").

Enjoying the service of tea in a private home was not an unexpected act of hospitality for us, but we *were* surprised to receive it in more public places like government offices, museums, hotel lobbies, ancient palaces, special mosques, small shops, or even on buses. We learned to enjoy and look forward to drinking tea and sharing conversation with others, even on the hot days of summer when temperatures reached more than 100 degrees.

Evie and friends are being served tea in an estekan by an Iranian professor.

As foreigners in Iran we had many opportunities to eat in the homes of strangers. This was especially true during the holy month of Ramadan—the ninth Islamic month of fasting in which Muslims believe the Quran was first revealed to the Prophet Muhammad.

Our first experience of Ramadan came soon after we had arrived in Iran. Our landlord's teenage daughter made special time to visit us in order to explain the meaning of Ramadan and the expectations for Muslims during this month. She explained that no one may eat, drink, or have sexual intercourse between sunup and sundown: "Not even a drop of water is permitted," she said. Those exempt from these requirements include persons who are old, sick, pregnant, nursing, traveling, or performing heavy manual labor. Instead, these persons are asked to feed the hungry. She invited us to join the community in celebrating this holy month and wanted to be our mentor, if we chose. We informed her that fasting is recommended in our faith as well and we would like to fast during the month but would follow different guidelines for fasting. A number of times she asked us about our fast and seemed pleased that we were honoring an important Muslim pillar of faith. Our experience of Ramadan was that it was an important time for spiritual awareness and for celebration. Following the day of fasting, friends, family, and neighbors break the fast by eating together and celebrating. Special foods and sweets are prepared just for this special month.

Our first experience of sharing a Ramadan meal in an unfamiliar home was an unforgettable experience. We had not eaten all day and were welcomed by our host and hostess who knew very little English (our skills in speaking and understanding Persian were very limited as well). We were invited to sit on the floor with members of the extended family, including grandparents, children, uncles, and aunts. The meal began with tea, dates, and walnuts. This was followed by a multiple-course meal of chicken, lamb, rice, eggplant, bread, and salad. Special desserts followed the main course: a special Ramadan pudding made with rosewater and saffron and pastries made only during Ramadan.

It was indeed a challenge for us to spend so much time eating on the floor, and we needed to change positions often to relieve the tingling in our legs or the burning pain in our hips. Our host noticed that Wally particularly was having difficulty sitting on the floor and recognized that this was not a familiar way for us to eat. He kept offering him a chair or a place at a table. Wally refused and said he would prefer to eat on the floor even though his hip tends to hurt a bit when he does.

Following the meal we retired to the living room and enjoyed sitting on soft sofas and chairs! Speaking together with broken English and Persian, we managed to get to know each other with the help of photographs and gestures. By the end of the evening we knew everyone's name and something about them. Our host loved poetry and had written many poems in calligraphy. He showed us some, as he knew we were enjoying the opportunity to learn and read Persian poetry.

We talked about the importance of peace between the United States and Iran. Visa restrictions and problems visiting these respective countries are seen as barriers to understanding one another. Our host remarked that our governments will never be able to make peace: "Peace comes from people like us getting to know one another." He continued, "It was important for me to realize you have pain in your hip when you sit on our carpets; I do too."

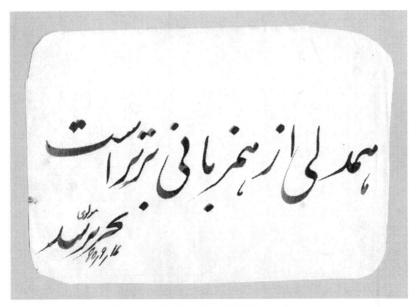

**Rumi's words in Persian: "Of shared heart or
shared tongue, shared heart is better."**

At one point in our conversation he got up from his chair and moved to his writing desk in the living room. He sat, took out a sharpened reed, dipped it into ink, and began to write. The room was silent. After some time he walked over to where we were sitting, carrying in his hands a beautifully written verse from the Persian poet Rumi (1207–73): "Of shared heart or shared tongue, shared heart is better." We struggled that evening to communicate through our *foreign* tongues but felt at ease through our *shared* hearts. That evening we learned that language need not separate us; deeper sharing occurs through the heart.

In addition to experiences of hospitality in homes and other more usual places, we also experienced hospitality in unusual and unexpected places, like the bus stop. It was a beautiful Thursday evening in the city of Qom. The moon was full, the weather balmy, the entire city bustling as we walked through crowded shopping areas. We moved quickly, weaving in and out of the crowds, stopping occasionally in small shops to admire the spices and nuts so beautifully arranged in large baskets.

As we passed a small fruit stand, the sight of fresh red apples reminded me of the need to buy some apples before we hurried off to catch a bus that would take us back to our small apartment. The owner of the store handed me a plastic bag, and I thanked him in my newly learned Persian. He smiled. I stooped beside a young Iranian woman and reached into the basket to gather several kilograms of apples. After filling the bag, I handed it to Wally and asked him to estimate the weight.

The woman beside me looked up and asked in English, "Where are you from?" It was quite startling to be spoken to in English! I told her that we were from the United States. Her face lit up, and she said that she was a student at one of the universities in Qom, studying to be an English teacher. She had never met or spoken to anyone from the United States and remarked that Iranians love the American English accent.

Her second question was very familiar, one we heard often: "Are you Muslim?"

"No," I replied, "I'm a Christian."

Surprised, she asked, "What is an American Christian doing in Iran?"

I explained that we were part of a student-exchange program designed to develop relationships of understanding and friendship between Muslims and Christians, Americans and Iranians.

We continued talking and sharing information about ourselves and our families. As our conversation ended and we shared our good-byes, I joined Wally to cross the busy intersection that would take us to the bus stop. Many people were waiting for the same bus we were to board. (In Qom, riding the bus is a challenge because men typically sit or stand in the front of the bus and women in the back. Because of this, Wally and I were not able to board or ride together.)

As we joined the waiting crowd at the bus stop, Wally stood with the men and I with the women, waiting and hoping there would be room for all of us on the bus. I stood out in that particular crowd, as I wore only a scarf and a lightweight coat while the other women were covered in the black chador.

Suddenly I felt a tap on my shoulder and turned to see the same student I had just talked to minutes before.

"Please excuse me," she said. "Could I speak with you for just a few more minutes?"

I left the crowd so I could talk with her.

"I was on my way back to my dormitory," she began, "and I kept thinking about our conversation. A question kept coming to my mind, and I knew I must ask you."

"Sure, what is it?"

"Aren't Iranians enemies of the Americans? Why have you decided to come and live with people who are your enemies?"

I put my hand on her shoulder and told her that we, and many Americans, do not consider the people of Iran to be our enemies. I shared with her how we have experienced firsthand the warmth and hospitality of the Iranian people.

A big smile covered her face, and she thanked me. "Another thing," she said. "I forgot to welcome you to my country. I will pray that your time here will be good and that you will be able to meet all your goals."

Then the already-crowded bus arrived and pulled to the curb. Wally walked to the front of the bus and took a seat. I waited in a line of women who were pushing and shoving to get on and soon realized there was no room for me. I quickly ran to the front and tapped on the window to tell Wally I would need to come on a later bus.

While I stood knocking on the window, my newfound friend ran to the front of the bus, grabbed my arm, and pulled me to the back. She spoke firmly yet gently to the women standing on the steps, asking of them, "Please, step off the stairs so our guest from America can ride home with her husband."

Every woman stepped off the steps and, with a spirit of graciousness, encouraged me to enter. As I stepped inside, an elderly woman seated in the front row stood up and insisted I take her place.

As the bus pulled away from the curb, tears were flowing down my cheeks. I somehow felt undeserving of such acts of kindness, such acts of hospitality. It made me wonder about how we in the United States treat guests from other countries. And the burning question of my student friend kept returning to my mind, asking for an honest response: "Why have you decided to come and live with your enemies?" Why was it we had decided to live in Iran with people some considered our "enemies"?

It wasn't an easy decision but a decision made with much discernment. Lying deeply within us was a hope that perhaps each conversation, each friendship, each act of kindness would help prepare the way for building a bridge of understanding, friendship, and even peace between two very different religions, between two very different countries.

Another unusual and unexpected place where we experienced hospitality was in a hotel in Esfahan. When we walked into the hotel, we were greeted with a tray of tea and bouquets of flowers. A poster hanging in the lobby offered these words of welcome, spoken by Imam Ali, son-in-law of the Prophet Muhammad: "As long as a tourist is in an Islamic country, the Islamic government is responsible to guarantee his safety and comfort. If a tourist in an Islamic country loses his property, the government should support and provide him with the lost property."

When we read these words of welcome with a group of learning-tour participants, we saw the words as well-meaning but likely not a reality. After several days touring Esfahan and adding several Persian carpets, miniature Persian paintings, hand-painted tablecloths, jewelry, and various crafts to our already-burdened suitcases, we checked out of our hotel rooms, climbed into our touring bus, and headed to the city of Shiraz.

After several hours of traveling, we stopped to visit a *caravanserai* (a roadside inn used hundreds of years ago by travelers in Iran). As we stepped out of the van, one of the tour participants realized he had left his billfold, passport, money, and several credit cards in his room at the Esfahan hotel. He looked through his luggage to double-check; they were nowhere to be found. Fear and anxiety were palpable in the group. How would he leave the country without a passport? What might have been charged on his credit card? He had no identification with him.

He had no doubt the cash would be gone but was most concerned about his passport and credit cards. We told our Iranian host of the situation, and he calmly said, "Don't worry, don't worry. I will call the hotel and tell them."

Our host, dressed in a flowing brown robe and white turban, took out his mobile phone and within minutes reached the hotel in Esfahan where we had stayed. All eyes were on him as he talked, looking for reassurance in his body language that all was well. Then he began to laugh, and the tension lowered significantly. He walked back to the group and reported that indeed the lost items had been found and would be waiting at the front desk to be picked up on our way back through Esfahan. Great relief swept over the group. On our return trip to the hotel, we picked up all the lost items; not a single penny was missing. "Love of stranger"—hospitality—shown to a vulnerable North American tourist! What was it that made us question the quotation of Imam Ali hanging on the hotel wall? That was a question that promoted honest self-searching.

It was in another hotel in the city of Shiraz where we were once again welcomed with tea and flowers as we entered to register. Another poster in the lobby caught our attention. This one read, "Feed everyone who enters this house, and don't ask about his faith, since anyone whose life is of worth to God, of course, is worthy of bread at Bolhasan's table." (It is thought that Bolhasan was the owner of a restaurant or hotel.)

Late in the evening, after touring the city, instead of going to a restaurant for supper, our tour group decided to eat in the hotel. In a table next to ours sat three young Iranian men who kept looking over at us. Finally, one of them got up from his seat and came to our table, asking where we were from and what we were doing in Iran.

He welcomed us with his broken English and then handed a blank sheet of paper to one of the tour group members, asking that he write on it what he believed. It seemed like a deep but very important question for this man, and he waited for a written reply.

The tour group member sat silently for several minutes, taking this request seriously. He responded: "I believe in love and compassion." The note was handed back to the young man and translated into Persian.

Taking it in his hand, he went back to the table where he was sitting earlier and began writing a response. When he had finished, he graciously handed the paper back and waited as it was translated into English. It read, "In the name of the holy. Honorable friend, I believe this, that we from all nations and countries are brothers and sisters."

What a profound and touching experience this was. True hospitality, true faith call us to receive people from all nations and all countries "as brothers and sisters."

We experienced great hospitality even from busy seminary students. Some of the streets in Qom are lined with bookstores. These bookstores are frequented by thousands of students from Iran and other countries who come to study Shia beliefs and practices in the dozens of seminaries in Qom.

Once a student has advanced to a certain academic level, he is granted permission to wear a turban: a white one for the usual student and a black one for those considered to be descendants of the Prophet Muhammad. The crowded sidewalks are dotted with the mostly white turbans.

I (Wally) learned to know a group of these seminary students, and one day they invited me to lunch with them in their dormitory. When the date for this lunch arrived, I made my way to their dorm and was invited in for tea and fruit, which we enjoyed on the carpets of their study room.

After some time of conversation, a cloth was spread out and food was served from the kitchen that was shared with several other rooms of students. I had expected a lunch, but to my surprise and delight they had prepared *fesenjan*, a famous deliciously rich dish of chicken cooked in walnut paste and pomegranate syrup.

Until this time, Evie and I had only eaten this food on very special occasions. We ate, talked, and finished with more fruit and tea. On my way back home they all walked with me for about two hundred yards. When at last they allowed me to walk on alone, one of them said, "We Iranians, we love our guests!"

Wherever we went and whenever we met people, we experienced abundant hospitality.

One day we left Qom in a taxi to visit the home of an important Iranian spiritual leader. We were graciously welcomed, and while savoring tea and fruit, we spoke of our recent reading of the Quran with one of our professors. Our host commended our effort, saying that a fresh reading of the Quran might reveal meanings that had not come to him.

It was a quiet and relaxing visit, and when we finally stood to leave, our host extended his hand. As he shook my hand, he said in Persian that the handshake is a symbol with roots many centuries old. He explained that a host would offer his guest the key to his city as a sign of friendship—a gesture from which the handshake later developed. Then our host added, "Today as I shake your hand I am giving you the key to my heart."

On another occasion in Qom, we had just concluded an evening of a shared meal, fruit, tea, and hospitable conversation. As I (Wally) stood to leave, the host told me in Persian, "You are in my heart." Then, as I was putting on my coat, the host repeated, "You are in my heart." And finally as we shook hands at his doorway, he said again, "You are in my heart." And to make certain I understood, with effort he repeated in his Iranian-English, "You are in my heart."

We also found something of this hospitality in the workplace.

The Iranian Red Crescent Society (IRCS) is the Iranian parallel of the American Red Cross. Mennonite Central Committee, with whom we were associated, had been doing collaborative work with IRCS since 1990.

One day we were visiting an IRCS orthopedic facility. While several of the staff were showing us around, I noticed the name badge of one of our hosts read *ruhnavaz*.

Since I was new to the Persian language, this name startled me. I knew *ruh* meant "spirit or soul" and *navaz* meant to "care for, cherish, or nourish." This man's name means "one who cares for the spirit"!

In my amazement I mentioned what I had noticed, and he responded proudly that indeed it was the meaning of his name. Several of his associates added that he was truly one who cares for the spirit of the patients with whom he works. I had to wonder what it would be like to live up to a name like that! In Iran it seemed like we were never far from the hospitality of the heart and the hospitality of the spirit: *ruhnavaz!*

Gift giving is another aspect of Iranian hospitality. When invited to another's home for a meal, a small gift (bouquet of flowers, chocolates, pastries, or nuts) is given to the hostess. Since we knew the importance of gift giving in the Iranian culture, we would encourage North American learning tour participants to pack small items to give to the Iranians they met while visiting in Iran.

One Canadian tour group member brought boxes of maple sugar, chocolate, and hand-blown glass moose and loons. She later shared her experience through this story:

> I gave one of the moose to Nesa, a twenty-three-year-old Iranian who had come to our hotel in Tehran to pick up a box of books I had brought for her. At least this is why I *thought* she had come by. But I was wrong. She came to give me gifts: homegrown spicy nuts, plump raisins, and fat pistachios for *all twelve* of the learning tour members, an elaborate mirror and an Iranian doll for my sister, who had sent her the books, and a fancy purse for me. Nesa

and I had never met before, and I was bewildered by the endless gifts she kept producing from her bag.

That's when I dived for the glass moose. Over the course of the day, Nesa accompanied our group to the National Museum in Tehran. In one of the display cases was a miniature bronze creature with big antlers. Nesa excitedly grabbed my arm: "Look! That's just like the one you gave me!" I laughed with delight to find a three-thousand-year-old Iranian equivalent to my Canadian moose. I felt a magical bond through history to the giver of that moose as I did to Nesa. Gifts do bind us to each other; the Iranians know this better than we do.

I soon realized that the real reason Nesa had shown up was that she came to be my friend. She stayed by me all day, explaining Iranian ways to me, waiting for me at exits if we got separated, translating for me, and showing a genuine interest in my family and home. Finally, she arranged for me to have a friend, Zahra, waiting for me when I arrived in Esfahan and another one, Nasrin, when I got to Qom. They, bearing beautiful gifts as well, totally embraced me and uncritically accepted me as their friend. *Would I have done that to a Muslim foreigner visiting my city?* I wondered. I will now![3]

Leading groups of North Americans through Iran led to the development of ongoing relationships and mutual exchanges of gift giving and receiving. Conversations with religious leaders, usually dressed in long robes and turbans, were important in building understanding and friendships. Our meetings always began by drinking tea together and eating lovely fruits, cucumbers, and pastries. This ritual seemed to put us at ease with one another.

One day we had arranged a meeting with a rather austere-looking religious leader who wanted our tour group to dialogue with him about our pacifistic stance. He challenged our viewpoints on a number of occasions. The discussion was lively and concluded when he said, "You are like nightingales: seekers of the beloved. You are welcome in my city. You are welcome to go anywhere you like in my city." As we stood to leave the room, we were handed bright green bottles of fresh olive oil and cups of hot tea. These gifts felt like an olive branch of peace and an offer of friendship.

As a stranger in a new culture, one must learn many new things, and learning often occurs in embarrassing ways. The tradition of gift giving was soon part of our life in Iran. When invited to a meal at someone's home, we remembered to take a gift; when returning to Iran after being in the United States, we filled our suitcases with small gifts for our friends.

However, there was one form of gift giving that was very strange for me (Evie). If a guest admired something an owner had and remarked about its beauty, the owner graciously handed it to the guest. Because of my ignorance of this cultural practice I became the embarrassed owner of jewelry, scarves, and perfume simply by expressing my delight in its beauty or scent.

When our student-exchange program came to an end, we began packing our suitcases to resettle back in the United States. The day before leaving, we carefully packed, knowing the weight restrictions our luggage would have. On the day of our departure, Iranian friends came to our apartment carrying gifts for our sendoff: small Persian carpets, pistachio nuts, Iranian candies, various Iranian crafts, books, Persian poems written on wooden plaques, tablecloths, and saffron. An older woman from northern Iran traveled eight hours by bus to send with us a special pastry we had enjoyed while visiting her home. It was overwhelming and delightful. The suitcases became unpacked and refilled with these beautiful gifts, which would continue to remind us of Iranian hospitality.

On our final ride to the Tehran airport we felt an odd assortment of emotions: excitement to be returning home, sadness to be leaving friends, tiredness from packing and saying good-byes, and blessed by the opportunities we had while living in Iran. We stepped out of the car accompanied by our friend and Iranian host, Dr. Haghani. He helped us pull our heavy suitcases into the airport and wanted to be sure we made it through the security checkpoints without difficulty. As we entered the crowded airport, a group of friends and teachers were waiting for us, wanting to say their final good-byes. In their arms were more gifts for our families at home: several pounds of pistachio nuts, Iranian candies, dried dates and figs. It was a sendoff never to be forgotten.

The Iranians certainly embodied a fresh understanding of the concept of hospitality, *philoxenia*—love of stranger—in our own Christian scriptures. In this way they were Christ to us. May we also be Christ to the strangers in our own homeland.

CHAPTER 3

Shared Heart, Shared Humanity

Human beings are members of one another
all created from the same precious jewel.
When, in the course of life,
pain comes to a member,
the other members cannot remain at peace.
When you do not grieve at the suffering of others
you cannot be called by the name "human."
—Persian poet Sa'adi Shirazi (1210–91)

This Persian poem is well-known throughout Iran and is on the tongue of nearly every Iranian. It is posted above an entryway at the United Nations building in New York. We *personally* experienced the empathetic care—the "humanity"—of the Iranians during our short stay in Iran. The following stories illustrate this.

We had lived in Iran only a month when the events of September 11 occurred. Like most people throughout the world, this day began as any other day. Our language teacher came to our apartment that afternoon, as expected, for a two-hour session of language study. Our language skills at this time were minimal. We knew quite a few Persian words, spoke short sentences, and understood more of the language than we could speak. Our teacher spoke only Persian so we never communicated in English. Nearly halfway through our lesson the telephone rang; it was the wife of our teacher, wanting to speak with her husband.

He took the phone, and before long we realized the conversation was a serious one, with many questions being asked. We understood some Persian phrases and were keenly aware of the serious expression of words used and facial expressions of concern. After some time, a concerned-looking teacher returned to the table and told us the United States had been "bombed."

Hearing the word "bombed" caused us great fear as we imagined bombs falling from planes over the United States. How would we know what had happened with such limited language skills? What about our family and friends? Were they safe? The television news would not be helpful as all news coverage at that time of day was in Persian.

Our teacher directed us to the living room sofa and turned on the television. We saw pictures of planes flying into the World Trade Center buildings and the disaster that followed, and we began to get a picture of what was happening in our country. We sat in disbelief, wondering how to respond. Soon our phone began ringing; friends and professors who spoke English called us to tell us exactly what was happening in the United States.

We felt so alone and devastated to hear the reports. Our teacher sensitively and caringly sat with us for the next hour, and we were comforted by his presence and willingness to be with us at this difficult time. The news of this event spread quickly throughout Iran, and within hours we received phone calls from students, neighbors, teachers, and friends throughout the country conveying their sorrow and asking how they might help us.

When suppertime arrived, an unknown neighbor knocked at our door and handed us a meal of chicken and rice. Soon after, another unknown neighbor knocked at our door. In his broken English he expressed deep sorrow for what had happened. He held in his hands a fresh, warm loaf of bread and humbly offered it to us: the bread of Christ—Eucharist—shared by our Muslim neighbor.

That night candles were lit around the country in honor of those who had died in this tragic event. We saw no dancing in the streets. The pain experienced in the United States was felt and honored by the Iranian people. We felt cared for through gifts of food, visits from both known and unknown friends, and frequent expressions of sympathy. The familiar words of the poet Saadi were realized: "When, in the course of life, pain comes to a member, the other members cannot remain at peace."

This empathetic care and compassion—this "shared humanity"—of our Iranian friends was offered to us again several months after we had returned home from our three-year assignment in Iran when Wally became very ill with an unknown virus and required hospitalization for nearly two weeks.

We wrote to our Iranian friends requesting their prayers for his recovery. We received daily e-mails from Iranian friends offering their thoughts and prayers on Wally's behalf. After his recovery we were told that one of our Iranian neighbors—one of our friends—had made a promise to God—a *nasr*—that if Wally was restored to health she would prepare a meal for fifty poor people who had difficulty buying wholesome foods. (In the Iranian tradition of nasr, a special request—like the request for Wally's recovery—is asked of God on behalf of another or of oneself. Accompanying the request is a vow that if God chooses to grant the request, a specific act of kindness would be carried out by the petitioner, such as offering food or money to the poor.) This friend carried out her promise by feeding more than fifty Afghan refugees.

Grieving over the suffering of others, even those who may not be of the same religion, culture, or family, bestows on us the honorable name *human*: *When in the course of life, pain comes to a member, the other members cannot remain at peace.*

We lived in Iran during the Israeli attacks on Gaza in early 2009. While visiting with the Iranian Red Crescent Society, the news of the attacks appeared on Iranian TV. People within the building poured into the waiting area to watch. Women wailed and children hugged the legs of their parents as they watched the tragedy unfold. The coverage of the attacks spared no sights of human suffering.

The following day we received a call from a young woman living in Tehran. She knew of our work with MCC and asked what our organization was doing to help with relief for the Palestinian people, especially women and children, who were suffering under such attacks. She said seeing the injured children was especially heavy in her heart and she wanted to respond but didn't know how.

We suggested one immediate response might be to write a prayer for the children and post it on her blog site. We later checked her blog and found the following prayer: "Watching the tears and suffering for you ... I am standing here ... there are thousands of kilometers of physical distance between us. I stretch my hand to catch yours ... you are there, too far to reach my hand. I am praying ... I am trusting my God ... PLEASE, SURVIVE!"

When in the course of life, pain comes to a member, the other members cannot remain at peace.

The Iranian Red Crescent Society (IRCS), along with other international relief organizations, played an important role in providing for the needs of refugees who had fled to Iran from surrounding countries. The individual Iranian people saw the plight of the Afghans and offered their personal acts of care and compassion—their *humanity*.

While visiting the home of an elderly woman in the city of Karaj, we noticed that after each meal she would leave the home carrying pots of food and bread. We had offered to help, not knowing where she was going or what she was doing, but she declined our offer. After several days we finally asked what she was doing. She said there was a construction site nearby and the workers were from Afghanistan. Their wages were low, and they had families to feed. While cooking meals she made enough to feed not only her family and guests but the Afghan workers as well. This she did quietly and humbly.

When in the course of life, pain comes to a member, the other members cannot remain at peace.

A young Iranian student lived near our apartment. We hadn't known him long before he began to talk to us about the many Afghans living in Qom who needed assistance with education and other things for their children. He took us to visit some of these refugees whom he had come to know. We were warmly invited into their homes to meet them and their families.

As we visited one home, other neighbors would come and ask that we visit them as well. At one point we went to the home of a thirty-year-old man dying from brain cancer. Medical care could no longer cure his illness. He was alone in his room and had no family members to care for him. He described the terrible headaches he dealt with daily and the narcotics that would not relieve the pain anymore.

He lay on the floor of a small room, bare except for the blankets on the floor, making for him a bed. Bandages were wrapped around his head, and with apparent pain he would try to turn his head to look at us. The young student knelt beside his floor bed, took his hand, and held it. Little was spoken between them.

There were no words to say, but the presence of a caring person meant much. Tears flowed down the face of the dying man. As we left his room, the student quietly put twenty dollars into the hand of his caretaker and said, "Use this money to pay for someone to come and sit with him. If you need more, here is my phone number." Tears of compassion fell down our faces as we witnessed a profound act of sharing the pain of another, the pain of one who was a stranger, yet a fellow human being "created from the same precious jewel."

When in the course of life, pain comes to a member, the other members cannot remain at peace.

Under the care of the IRCS, hundreds of displaced Afghans lived in tents close to the Iranian border and were given various forms of aid, such as housing, fresh water, cooking equipment, and minimal food supplies. Several months after the events of September 11, we were able to travel with IRCS staff to see this work being carried out in an effort to relieve some of the suffering experienced by the Afghan people.

We felt a mixture of emotions when we departed from Zahedan, Iran, to visit one of these refugee camps managed by the IRCS. We felt a sense of adventure traveling into Taliban-ruled areas and the unknown, as well as a sense of sadness as we thought about bombs exploding in Afghanistan with the loss of lives, people fleeing to avoid the attacks, and destruction of land and resources. As we neared the Afghan border, moments of fear raised our heart rates. Since we were accompanied by several IRCS workers, it was much easier to pass the police checkpoints and enter Afghanistan.

The countryside was desert: flat, dusty, dry, stony, and windy with no signs of plant life. Occasionally we would pass a camel lying dead beside the road. We followed a riverbed that was completely dry.

In the distance, about four kilometers from the Iranian border, we saw rows of tents in neat lines, clouded by the dust. Iranian Red Crescent Society flags were flying high on each side of the road leading into the camp area. Nearly six hundred displaced Afghans were living in the camp, many of whom were children.

We stopped and stepped out onto the dusty, rocky earth. We were immediately greeted with "salam" from both old and young— "peace" spoken to *us* by those whose country had been invaded by and was at war with our country.

Many children gathered around and followed us as we toured the camp. We were shown the water supply—huge tanks of water carried in daily by trucks. Women washed clothes, and a few children played in little puddles here and there. A generator supplied electricity to the tents. Numerous small bathrooms were available, and the men of the camp were busy building additional bathrooms of clay and brick.

Each family was housed in a sturdy tent with ground cover. Blankets and cooking utensils were provided. As we walked around the camp, more and more children joined us and giggled as they engaged us in speaking Persian with them.

They told us stories of leaving their homes and coming to the camp, which was very difficult. They missed their schools, friends, and family members. They talked of having rice, beans, and bread but no meat and not enough milk. Fruits and vegetables were rare. Most of their shoes had worn out walking over the rocks and stones to get to the camp. One young girl reported that the children missed going to school and had no books, tablets, or pencils.

As we walked and talked, one young boy turned to me and said, "You're from America, aren't you?"

**Evie and several Iranian Red Crescent Society staff meet with
the children and displaced families living in Afghanistan.**

I felt awkward and ashamed to admit that I was from the very country that took them from their homes, friends, schools, and families—that *caused* their personal pain and displacement. "I am living in Iran now," I replied.

But he was persistent. "But you're really from America."

I told him I was from America *and* that we were here to visit and help his people by sending food, blankets, and money. He was quiet, and we walked several minutes without talking.

As we walked with our heads down, my eye caught sight of a beautiful, polished stone, and I stooped to pick it up. Then I saw another and also reached for it. The children looked carefully at me and a few stepped back. What might they be thinking? I chose my words carefully. "I would like to take these stones back to my home so I can look at them every day and remember you. I never want to forget this experience of being with you here in Afghanistan. Would you give me permission to take them with me?"

The children looked at one another, smiled, and nodded their approval.

An IRCS staff member interrupted us at that point and said we were to meet for a short meeting. I left the children and joined the staff. We met together in one of the family tents and were seated on the dirt floor. Tea was served as we talked. The staff expressed concern about a prolonged war and wondered how they could possibly care for more refugees who would surely be making their way to safety here.

They looked tired but frequently laughed together. We told them about our assignment in Iran and our willingness to supply various forms of assistance, through Mennonite Central Committee, that would help them in caring for these many displaced persons. They seemed pleased.

After nearly thirty minutes of conversation we began to hear voices outside the tent. They were children's voices that grew louder and louder. One of the workers got up and quickly walked to the door of the tent. I heard him say, "She doesn't want those dirty stones!"

I immediately got up and saw a group of nearly thirty children, each one holding a beautiful stone. All the children remained silent, but their eyes met mine. "Where did you get those beautiful stones?" I asked. They told me they had run to the farthest borders of the camp to find the most beautiful ones and wanted me to have them.

As I stood at that tent door, each child came up to me one by one. Each gently put a stone that he or she had found in my hands and told me his or her name. I then dropped the stone into a pocket I made in my long coat. When they finished, I held in my coat at least thirty smooth, polished stones from the Afghanistan desert.

I thanked these children and shared my delight at being the recipient of such beautiful stones. "You know what I would like to do with these stones?" I asked. "I would like to take them back to the United States with me and give them to children in my country so they can also remember you. Would that be okay?"

They eagerly answered that they would like that.

When I reentered the tent, the workers groaned and wanted to know if I really wanted to carry all those stones with me; I assured them I did.

Since then, I have reflected many times on this gift of stones given by the Afghan children—shared heart, shared humanity— and on the work of the IRCS in providing for the needs of their hurting neighbors. Iranian hospitality crosses international borders to meet the needs of the most vulnerable of the world, yet rarely is this kindness recognized by the larger international community.

When in the course of life, pain comes to a member, the other members cannot remain at peace.

CHAPTER 4

Persian Carpets—Weavers of Dialogue

Trust, enhanced by acceptance of our common humanity, laid the foundation for dialogue with our Iranian friends, who were always eager to share conversations with us. One night we stepped inside the door of some friends' home. When we took off our shoes, our feet were embraced by their Persian carpets.

Our host welcomed us, saying, "Please sit with us on our carpets, drink tea, and eat fruit with us; we love to talk!" This invitation to dialogue commonly greeted us as we visited both friends and strangers in Iran.

As we left the home of another family, following a good meal and much conversation, our Iranian host said, "Our governments will never be able to bring peace to our two nations. It is only by people like us, getting to know each other and understanding our common humanity, that peace will come."

Similarly, one of our Iranian professors said, "We need to take dialogue forward, and then we can appear before God and say we did our best." He then illustrated his point by the following story from the Persian poet Rumi: A certain man gave a unit of currency, called a *dirham*, to a group of four people. One of them, a Persian, said, "I will spend this on *angur* [the Persian word for *grape*]." The second one, an Arab, said, "No, I want *inab* [the Arabic word for *grape*], not *angur*, O rascal!" The third, a Turk, said, "This money is mine. I don't want an *inab*; I want *uzum* [the Turkish word for *grape*]." The fourth, a Greek, said, "Stop this talk! I want *istafil* [the Greek word for *grape*]."

In their folly, these four people, representing various languages, lands, and cultures, began to fight with one another, striking each other with their fists. They were full of ignorance and empty of knowledge. If a master of the esoteric—a revered and many-languaged person—were there, she or he would have pacified them. She or he would have said, "With this one *dirham* I will give all of you what you wish."[4]

This story reminds me (Evie) of a personal encounter I had while speaking to a US church group about Islam and Christianity. An older gentleman was in the audience, and I could sense that he was becoming very agitated as I spoke. During a time of response he stood up and with a loud, shaking voice said, "Allah and God are not the same. Allah is an idol that Muslims worship, not the God of Christianity."

I explained that the word "Allah" is an Arabic word for God and used by Muslims in addressing God. I later took the opportunity to talk with him more about our different understandings and to listen to his concerns. As our conversation came to a close, he became tearful and said that he had spoken out of ignorance and needed to study this more.

Like Rumi's tale about the four people asking for grapes in their respective languages, none understanding the other, the lack of understanding around our nuanced ways of speaking about the divine is a barrier that too often blocks dialogue and causes violence. Once we learn to speak another's language, we begin to understand that our apparent differences are simply that—*apparent* but not necessarily so.

In reflecting on sharing life with the Iranians, the dominant image that comes to mind is sitting together on lovely Persian carpets and spending hours together in conversation. One of the most well-known and highly praised Iranian exports is the Persian carpet, a product of Iran for more than twenty-five hundred years. Persian carpets, both handmade and machine-made, are found in mosques, offices, museums, and nearly every home. We were always fascinated when we would walk into Iranian homes and find a large loom in the main area of the home with a carpet in progress, both children and adults taking part in its making.

The quality of the carpet depends on the number of knots per square centimeter, ranging from thirty- to fifty-plus, with the number of knots corresponding to the price of the carpet (i.e., the more knots per square centimeter, the higher the price). As we studied the making and the use of the Persian carpets, we found it to be an appropriate metaphor for the dialogue we experienced in Iran. We saw the Weaver (God) as one who interlaced various sets of threads, creating a web of fabric that was much more than the sum of its parts. Our different voices became the threads weaving back and forth in dialogue, creating the art of understanding.

A silk Persian carpet is being woven in the home of an Iranian family.

Before going to Iran we read many articles and books on dialogue, as we knew dialogue would be an important aspect of our assignment and one we needed to understand more fully. Among other questions, we asked ourselves, "What does dialogue involve? And when is a conversation with another considered *dialogue*?"

Dialogue within the context of faith includes listening and sharing with deep sensitivity so that each person may be able to represent the meaning of what the other has shared. The goal of the dialogue is not to change another's belief, but to offer authentic sharing and respectful listening. When we experienced this type of dialogue among our Muslim friends, we sensed deep mutual respect.

An Iranian professor at the Iranian Academy of Philosophy and Religious Studies made the following helpful comment: "True dialogue begins only when one has learned to listen. The first step in a real dialogue is the very difficult task of listening, for it is only through listening that the listener will be truly able to speak." (Perhaps the foundational threads on the Persian carpet loom represent the listening aspects of dialogue and the colorful threads knotted onto the foundation represent the voice that arises in response to careful listening.)

A common way of thinking about dialogue within the context of faith includes the dialogue of life, the dialogue of collaboration, theological dialogue, and spiritual dialogue. Following are some stories illustrating our Iranian experience of these types of dialogue.

The Dialogue of Life

This involves sharing all aspects of life and living together, with its goal being mutual understanding and appreciation. Through the sharing of daily life it becomes apparent that we share a common humanity consisting of pain and joy, new life and death, peace and turmoil, tears and laughter. As the experience of our common humanity is shared, trust develops, which is foundational to further levels of dialogue.

Celebrating holidays and religious holy days were memorable times in Iran and an opportunity to share in the dialogue of life. Throughout our years in Iran, both Christian and Islamic holy days were shared together in mutual appreciation.

The Christmas season was a time when I (Evie) anticipated feelings of loneliness and homesickness. The absence of Christmas music, lights, decorated Christmas trees, nativity scenes, and Santa Claus was a stark reminder of our differences in cultures. I wondered how to celebrate this important holiday in Iran. I tried to put a few things in our apartment to remind us that we were in the season of Christmas: lights, a card with Mary and Jesus, wrapped gifts, candles, and a few meaningful ornaments hanging here and there.

On one particular Christmas day I remember feeling like it was a very ordinary day instead of a special holy day to be celebrated. We went to our classes as usual, shopped in the market for our daily food, and studied our Persian lessons. In the afternoon as I sat at the table studying, our doorbell rang. When I opened the door, a friend whom I had been meeting with weekly appeared, holding in her hand a beautiful bouquet of flowers.

"Isn't this the day Christians celebrate the birth of Jesus?" she asked.

"Yes," I replied and invited her in.

This friend had just come from a flower shop where she had given the florist specific instructions on how to make a Christmas bouquet. It contained a special flower in Iran called Maryam, named after Mary, mother of Jesus. There were greens and a red rose, as she said she had remembered Jesus was sometimes referred to as a rose. Accompanying the bouquet was a Christmas card portraying an icon of Mary and Jesus and these words: "We celebrate with you the birth of Jesus, loved by both Christians and Muslims." Later on that day a young student called us and wondered if he and his wife might visit us later in the evening since this was Christmas day and they did not want us to feel alone on this special day. They arrived at nine p.m. carrying wrapped gifts, pistachios, and cotton candy, to be shared together.

"We weren't sure what you ate on Christmas, but we knew presents were part of your tradition," they remarked. We sat together on our Persian carpet talking and listening as we shared the meaning of Christmas in both our religious traditions. Each Christmas season our Muslim neighbors joined us in a Western-style Christmas dinner, bringing gifts and friendship.

In addition, students at the institute were always eager to learn about holiday traditions in the United States and were eager to make us feel at home by honoring some of our holiday customs with us. Some of the students had never met an American, but many students had family members living in the United States who shared holiday customs with them.

Two young men from the institute were eager to visit us one Christmas day and were trying to think what might be an appropriate gift to bring. They had heard that cake was an important part of Christmas dinner, so they went to a bakery to buy a cake. They wanted it to represent, in some way, an aspect of Christmas. They called to tell us of their coming, and we met them at our apartment door; they were carrying a box.

"Christmas greetings," they offered. "May we come in?"

When these students entered, they remarked how hard it must be to be away from home on this special day, so they wanted to share part of the day with us. "We wanted to bring you a Christmas cake," they said, "but didn't know what a Christmas cake should look like." They went on to say that they had visited a bakery and asked the baker if he knew what Christians would put on a Christmas cake; this baker had no idea. So they tried another baker and again the baker said he could be of no help.

On the third try they found a baker who said his family lives in the United States and he knew about Christmas cakes. They were delighted and bought the cake. They were excited to put the cake on the kitchen table and watched us open it. As we lifted the lid, we were greeted with the face of none other than *Donald Duck*!

"Do you like it?" they asked.

"Yes!" we replied, as we cut the cake and shared it around the table.

The Islamic holiday of Ashura (a holiday commemorating the martyrdom of Imam Hussein, grandson of the Prophet Muhammad, more than thirteen hundred years ago) is a very important time for Shia Muslims. Several days are set aside each year for this commemoration and holiday. Thousands of people in nearly every city in Iran gather in the streets chanting, "Hussein! Hussein! Hussein!"

The holiday of Ashura celebrated in the city of Karaj.

Groups of men and boys march, beating drums, pounding their chests, and chanting. The buildings are draped in black banners. At various sites the story of Imam Hussein and his martyrdom is told or enacted. People weep as they are reminded of the imam's horrible death and the death of those in his family.

All along the street people serve tea and various foods, free of charge, in honor of the imam. Many taxi drivers drive without fees.

Each year during Ashura we were invited to share in these celebrations and to learn more about an imam who refused to sacrifice important Islamic beliefs and instead accepted death.

As the holiday of Ashura illustrates, sharing the dialogue of life also involves sharing the dialogue of death. Though the outward expressions of grief at the time of death may vary from person to person and culture to culture, the feelings are very much the same. The following story illustrates this.

We were fortunate to have as a neighbor a Muslim cleric named Abbas who would visit several times weekly, stopping by to ask how we were doing, or sit with us at the table to discuss issues of religion, politics, or life in general. This neighbor had a family of six young children who followed their father's example and befriended us as well. They were eager to help us learn Persian and hoped we could teach them English.

One afternoon a neighbor called and told us that Abbas had died suddenly of an apparent heart attack. We were encouraged to go to the home and join the grieving family members and friends. Only these few words were necessary, we were told: "We express to you our sorrow."

We walked to our friend's home, saddened by his death and uneasy about cultural expectations at such a time. As we walked into the house, Abbas's elderly mother was seated on the floor crying out, "God, where are you?" She cried for her son to return. "Abbas, come back. I am your mother, come."

Abbas did not return home, but during this time of intense grieving, pleas for God's presence were voiced, as well as affirmations that Abbas was "in a better place than this, in Paradise." Common Arabic phrases, *"Allah akbar, Allah akbar"* ("God is greater") rang from various corners of the room along with, *"Allah al-rahman, al-rahim"* ("God the compassionate, the merciful").

Abbas's grief-stricken wife wailed for reassurance that he was in the hospital and had not died. We had no words to comfort, but we sat silently and joined others in the grieving. In the days that followed we continued to mourn the loss of Abbas and wondered how we might comfort his grieving family. I (Evie) decided to write a tribute to him outlining what I had learned from him. These were my thoughts.

"Don't let this turban scare you." In the first encounter we had with Abbas, Abbas came to visit us in his usual clerical clothing—a long black robe and a white turban wrapped neatly around his head. I felt a bit intimidated, which he must have sensed, for he quickly said with his usual sense of humor, "Don't let this robe and turban scare you; it is just our dress here, you know." I thought about how often we allow clothing, skin color, nationality, or position to "scare us" or determine who our friends will be. Such external things may keep us from initiating friendships with people of other races, cultures, and religions.

Offer a hand of friendship. Before living in Iran, one of the things I was taught was *not* to offer my hand to a man but to shake hands only if a man first offers me his hand. Abbas was one of a few men who did offer me his hand, and when he did, I felt it to be a sign of warmth and acceptance, and tears filled my eyes. Later in our relationship I thanked him for this, and he told me that when we live with people of other cultures, it is important to remember that some things simply are cultural, not faith-bound.

Be generous, seek justice. The first year of our life in Iran, when our Persian language skills were minimal, I learned a lot about Islam by watching people. One day, before a visit back to the Unites States, I asked Abbas to accompany me to the market to buy several small Persian carpets to take back to friends and family as gifts. I knew if I went alone the prices would be much higher. Abbas quickly agreed to accompany me and we went to a little shop, hidden in a dark corner of the market.

A man showed us a small carpet that his wife had spent nearly a year making. He was a student from Afghanistan and the father of several small children. His wife had made the carpet to help the family earn a living. He quoted a price to us. I waited for Abbas to begin bargaining with him for a lower price. Instead, he turned to me and said he did not feel comfortable asking for a lower price, knowing the circumstances of this man. "In fact," he said, "the price he is asking is not adequate for the time his wife has spent working on this. It would really be better to pay more." He was right, and I greatly admired his integrity and readiness to seek a just wage for this family.

Disagreements will not interfere with continued friendship. We did not agree with Abbas on everything and shared different points of view on various issues. Some of these issues concerned the need for war, the role of women in a society, Jesus's identity, and human rights. We both spoke honestly about our own beliefs but also listened carefully as the other spoke. Our disagreements never kept Abbas away. We agreed to disagree on certain issues and found that underneath our disagreements was a commitment to a relationship that was much deeper than the differences expressed.

Be passionate and authentic. Abbas was passionate about many things, including his faith in God, and in the midst of a discussion he would frequently walk over to our bookshelf, pull out the Quran, and read us a certain verse. Or he would get up from his chair, walk over to the blackboard in our living room, and with markers clarify his point of view. "Now what do you think?" he would ask. He would then take his seat and quietly listen as we responded. He was eager to share his understanding of God and was eager to learn new ways of understanding.

Abbas's invitation to share authentically from his own beliefs and experiences encouraged us to share a difficult part of our own lives. During the years we were living in Iran, our daughter Kristy and her husband struggled with infertility in the form of multiple and recurrent miscarriages. I (Evie) shared my pain around this with a number of my Iranian friends and through my sharing experienced a common bond of understanding and empathy. Several people committed themselves to pray for our daughter. One of our teachers even made a trip to the holy city of Mashhad to purchase a special salt that was known to help women who had problems carrying a pregnancy. We were frequently asked how she was doing.

As a result of her frequent miscarriages, our daughter decided to adopt a daughter from China. We shared this decision and celebrated the adoption with our Iranian friends. Adoption is not common in Iran, and many were eager to hear this story and understand more about the motivation to adopt a child from another country. As a result of our dialogue around this, our Iranian friends began to question why adoption is not more common in Iran.

This was an important opportunity to discuss our different practices and to share our common pain. In response to my vulnerability of sharing this personal pain around infertility, other Iranian women experiencing infertility problems would often come to talk to me. In this way I too was given the opportunity to pray for those with whom I could share a similar sort of pain and loss.

Another aspect of interfaith dialogue that we experienced in Iran was the dynamic existing between the Muslim population, the huge majority, and the Christian population, a tiny minority. In fact, the number of Christians in Iran is less than one-half of 1 percent of the total population.

An underlying issue is the possibility of Muslims becoming Christian. One of our Islamic scholar friends acknowledges this dynamic by saying that if the number of Christians would double in the next twenty years, the government would not do anything to stop the increase. However, he went on to say that a religion does not like to lose its members. Another of our Islamic scholar friends agrees that the government would not forbid change, but he would go on to say that the government does promote incentives for Muslims to remain Muslim and disincentives for Muslims to become Christian. He adds further that it is mostly the families who provide the pressure for its members to remain Muslim.

Of the Christians in Iran, the large majority are members of the Armenian Orthodox Church. One of our Orthodox Christian friends acknowledges this dynamic, and the following is a paraphrase of what he had to say. "We have our language, our own social and cultural institutions; our women do not have to wear hijab in our own buildings, and we get along tolerably well with the government."

Our friends among the more evangelical Christian churches, particularly those who conduct their church service in the Persian language, see these dynamics from a much different perspective. The following is a paraphrase of a conversation with one of our evangelical Christian Iranian friends. "I admire what you [Evie and Wally] are doing to dialogue with Iranian Muslims in the city of Qom. I wish I could do the same but we are so tired. We spend our energy protecting ourselves and we don't think about dialogue with our Muslim counterparts. We have built walls to protect ourselves. For instance, a young Iranian calls by phone asking about Christianity. What can I do? The government forbids us from responding to calls like this. Can you imagine what this is like, not being able to openly discuss our faith with someone searching? And we have to stop and think, *This may be someone calling for the government to see how we will respond.* There are those who become Christians and want to participate in the life of the church but we have to caution them of the dangers for both them and for us. Many remain secret Christians. They usually do okay until their children go to school. Then it becomes very difficult and many eventually leave Iran."

For us, dialogue meant listening: to the pain of our friends; to the complexity of human interaction; to the years of what has gone before, and for the hope of God's kingdom coming.

The dialogue of collaboration. A second form of dialogue we experienced while living in Iran is the dialogue of collaboration. Bonds of unity are established through the process of living and working together with those of a different culture and religion. Here again, through bringing together different ideas and weaving them together in collaboration, one is able to accomplish something he or she could not do alone.

During the first year in Iran, I felt the need to become involved in something other than studying. My life in the United States was a busy one, with involvements in many different projects and programs. I wished to do something that would allow me to be involved with the lives of other women and the lives of the poor.

I made my wishes known to the director of our learning program, and he introduced me to an organization of women who met several times weekly to sew for economically disadvantaged families. I found myself at the sewing machine with women of all ages and various opinions about women "from the West."

Some were a bit surprised that I knew how to sew, as they thought women in the United States valued only professional skills, not domestic ones. As we worked together to make potholders, shirts, clothing for children, and other items, we not only provided valuable products for the poor but learned much about each other.

Conversation flowed easily as we worked together. "Are you afraid living in Iran?" one of the women asked me one day.

All machines stopped to hear my reply. "Why no," I replied. "I have never felt afraid to walk the streets alone at night or to be alone at home. I have felt very safe here."

"*Alhamdulillah*," they responded together. "Praise God."

At times we struggled with the limited number of sewing machines, or finding scissors that would cut fabric, or a needle that was sharp enough to penetrate the cloth. We talked about how to make the sewing room more efficient.

On one of my return trips home I discussed our sewing situation with our home congregation, which was eager to find helpful ways of joining us in our efforts in Iran. I suggested that perhaps the congregation might make sewing kits for each of the women working in the sewing room and with the kit write a note expressing a desire for peace and better relationships between our countries.

The congregation eagerly took the idea and ran with it. Twenty kits were made, which included not only sewing supplies but letters and chocolates. I translated the letters into Persian and distributed them when I returned to Iran. The joy and excitement of the women at receiving such unexpected gifts was something to behold. How I wish I could have captured that moment! A small effort of collaboration soon spread and grew like a mustard seed.

We had another experience where we had the opportunity to collaborate with the Iranian Red Crescent Society on projects that provided relief for those experiencing natural disasters or for refugees cared for by the IRCS.

One of the projects was to provide prostheses for Afghans who lost limbs due to detonated cluster bombs and land mines remaining from years of Soviet occupation and civil war. On a trip to the city of Zahedan we were able to see the efforts of our collaboration make a difference in the lives of several Afghan refugees. Jamieh Hashmi was one. The story below is a story about her life, which she shared with me.

Jamieh Hashmi

I was born about eighteen years ago in a small village outside Kabul, Afghanistan. I am the oldest of eight children. I have four sisters and three brothers. My father worked as a shepherd, but he was killed when

I was only eight. That changed my life a lot because as the oldest I had to take over my father's work.

Each morning I would get up at first light so I could take our family's six sheep to the pasture. I would spend each morning out in the pastures caring for our sheep. We lived in the desert and it was hard to find food for them. I walked over rocks and hills looking for something the sheep might eat. I could not attend school because I had to help my family.

Each day was pretty much the same for me until I was eleven. One day, while trying to find food and water for our sheep, I was thrown to the ground by a terrible blast. I didn't know what had happened. I saw only blood and broken bones in my leg. Later I was told that I had stepped on an unexploded bomb. My younger brother was with me; he left me with the sheep while he ran for help.

I stayed in the hospital for the next two months. My leg could not be saved and had to be cut off below my right knee. I left the hospital without my leg. Because of the help our family received from the IRCS, I was able to get an artificial leg. We had no money to pay for it ourselves.

Life in Afghanistan was difficult, and because of the war with the Taliban we moved to the village of Namat Abad in Iran. That was several years ago.

I got married, and five months ago my daughter, Hava, was born. She was delivered by my mother at home because we had no money to go to the hospital. My troubles continued after she was born for my breasts dried up and I could not feed her. We now must buy milk for her.

It has been difficult for me since I lost my leg. I feel very sad. One leg is shorter than the other and I still feel pain. On three different occasions the foot of my artificial leg has broken and I have had to seek help again from the IRCS.

This is why I am here today, to get my broken foot repaired. It is not easy for us to get here. We travel in a minibus over rough, unsafe roads. But I must get my leg fixed because I cannot do my work without it. I cannot care for my daughter without my leg.

I don't know about the future. I would like to return to Afghanistan someday, but we have no money to do so. We do not have enough to buy milk for Hava today.[5]

Jamieh's story was deeply touching to those of us who collaborated to make life for her a bit easier. Together we discussed ways to provide her with an ongoing milk supply for Hava and continued help with her prostheses. The end result of this collaborative process hopefully improved the life of one family.

Theological dialogue. Theological dialogue was often present for us in Iran because in Iran religion is an important part of everyday life. In nearly every conversation some aspect of religion, faith, or theology would arise. The purpose of theological dialogue is to see and to understand theological concepts through the eyes of another. The outcome of such dialogue is unknown if one enters it with openness and integrity.

In our personal experience, theological dialogue with Iranian friends transformed our own faith. In fact, our Muslim friends have been most helpful to us in living out our faith and beliefs, pointing out our hypocrisies, or inviting us to see theological differences as areas of personal growth.

One of the richest experiences I (Evie) enjoyed in Iran was a weekly Bible study focusing on the gospel of Luke with the director of a women's seminary in Qom. This was a sacred time for me as I engaged new understandings of a familiar text with my Muslim friend.

When we reached the twelfth chapter of the book—the chapter in which Jesus warns against the hypocrisy of the Pharisees and tells the parable of the rich fool—our study time was nearly up when Mahnaz began to gather her notes and prepare to leave.

"Wait," I said, "would you have time for just one more section of this chapter? It is so beautiful and a good note to leave on."

"Why not?" she answered. So we read Jesus's comforting words about God's care for the birds and flowers, the invitation to put worries aside, to trust in God's loving care, and the commandment to consider the lilies.

As Mahnaz prepared to leave, I commented that these verses have been a great source of strength to me in my spiritual journey.

"They are indeed beautiful verses," she remarked.

Mahnaz returned the next week to continue our studies. We usually began by sharing how we and our families were doing, where we were finding joy, and where we were struggling. When it was my turn to share, I expounded on how worried I was about our visas coming through for an upcoming women's learning tour. I pointed out all the holidays ahead when the foreign ministry office would be closed and how little time remained to get the visas approved.

Mahnaz listened intently, gently closed the calendar I was holding, and began to chuckle. I looked at her in surprise. Did she not understand?

"Evie," she said gently, "let's read again those beautiful words of Jesus about not needing to worry. The visas are now in God's hands, not in yours, and we must now just wait and trust."

I was taken aback by my own blindness and hypocrisy. I thanked Mahnaz and remarked that her words and reassurance were the very reason I needed someone like her to walk with me in my own journey of faith, to lovingly point out my own blind spots.

As a part of the student-exchange program, we had the opportunity to participate in more formal theological dialogue, since one of the key initiatives in the exchange program was interfaith bridge building. In 2009 a seminar was held in Iran on the topic "Peace and Justice: Mennonite and Shiite Perspectives in Dialogue."

The conference was held over a three-day period, during which scholars from both religious traditions could learn from each other, develop mutual understandings, and establish ongoing friendships. Papers were presented based on the theological understandings of the two religious traditions. Between sessions time was allowed for participants to engage in many private conversations.

The Muslims and Mennonites involved in this dialogue experienced a clear sense of who they were as Muslims and as Christians. According to Dr. Ed Martin, former MCC director of the Iran program, "Our Muslim counterparts also believe that by engaging in interfaith dialogue they can sharpen their own faith and expand their understanding of God, while at the same time increase their understanding of 'the other' and build new friendships." In addition to formal discussions and time for private conversations participants traveled together to important cities and sites within Iran in order to experience the culture of the other.

Evie with her friend Khatoon in the city of Kashan.

While we lived in Iran, there were numerous opportunities to dialogue about religion and theology, and many significant conversations took place very unexpectedly. One of our Iranian friends, Khatoon, was a professor who also was fluent in English and had majored in English literature. Whenever she visited, I would send with her English books I thought she might enjoy that we could later discuss.

On one of her visits, I gave her *The Faith Club,* a story about a Muslim woman, a Christian woman, and a Jewish woman searching together for understanding of the other's religion. After reading the book she called, inviting me to visit. I made plans to travel to her home thinking this was an ordinary, friendly visit.

I barely settled into her home when she said we must sit down and talk. She was abounding in energy and questions after reading the book. "Evie," she said, "what makes you a Christian? Are you a Christian because you were born to Christian parents? Tell me now, what must you say or do to be called Christian? I know you must believe in Jesus, but I believe in Jesus too, so does that make me a Muslim/Christian? It is very easy to know what makes me a Muslim. I must only say that there is one God and that Muhammad is God's prophet. I was born Muslim. Help me understand what it means to be called Christian."

She sat on the edge of her chair totally engaged in our conversation. And then came the common question we were asked so many times, "Why do Christians believe in three gods? I just can't understand your beliefs about the Trinity."

She also begged to understand why, after studying Islam for several years and studying the life of the Prophet Muhammad, I still decided to identify as a Christian. "What is it about Jesus that you find different from our prophet?" Many similar questions followed, and I found myself tiring as I attempted to share my answers with her.

"Khatoon," I said, "do you realize you have been focusing on all our different understandings of faith? We share many common beliefs, which you haven't mentioned."

"Oh," she replied, "it's our differences that make us stretch and grow in our understandings. The differences challenge us to think in new ways and enlarge faith. Similarities don't do that. Our differences are treasures!"

Khatoon's words and passion produced new stirrings within me that made me ask how it is that one finds a "treasure" in different beliefs and understandings. Her response caused me to look at myself and the fact that I feel some dis-ease when conversations focus on differences. I hadn't thought of differences being a treasure before.

As our conversation came to a close, I was grateful to see differences as "treasure," a treasure waiting to be found, unlocked, and necessary to enlarge my thinking and faith. We took a walk in a nearby park following our intense conversation and together suddenly realized that God also is one who loves differences as we observed the many varieties of spring flowers and the different phases of the opening buds.

During a visit to Iran in January 2006, Wally attended a conference at the Institute for the Study of Religions and Sects at Qom on the topic of interfaith dialogue. During the conference, one of the presenters made the comment that Islam was a more complete religion than Christianity. Wally asked him about this, but he didn't have time for a complete answer.

Several days later Wally had a long car ride with a highly respected Islamic scholar and asked him about this matter. This scholar responded that one could not judge this matter from the perspective of inner purity, closeness, and dependence on God but from the perspective of a religion's positive effect on its society. He continued, "Islam has a divinely revealed law that helps govern affairs of society and in this respect it may be a more complete religion. But," he said, "I am not certain about this."

This scholar went on to say that the most important aspect of religion was to live in this world as if under the rule of God and not rely on salvation as a gift that allows one to disregard life on earth. He added that salvation is living a life of salvation here and now.

He concluded his remarks by saying that, according to Allamah

Tabatabai, the modern Shia interpreter of the Quran, if a person of any faith lives according to the knowledge of God that has been revealed within his or her faith tradition, there is not fault within that person. If, however, that person disregards the knowledge of God and God's desire for his or her life, then there is fault no matter what religion he or she follows. If a person of one faith knows that another faith is nearer the Truth, he or she must not disregard this knowledge; to do so would be a fault with him or her.

This response demonstrates two characteristics of interfaith dialogue: the importance of stating one's own understanding of one's faith and being open to truth that may lie beyond one's faith.

As leaders of several learning tours to Iran, we arranged for participants to dialogue with government representatives, university professors, Armenian Christians, seminary professors, religious leaders, and a variety of other Iranians. While in the city of Shiraz, one specific tour group met with a representative of the Supreme Leader for the province of Fars who was the leader of Friday prayers in Shiraz.

We were ushered into a room where news reporters and TV cameras were stationed to broadcast our meeting. We were introduced as a group of Christians from the United States and Canada seeking to bring about peace in the world.

This Muslim leader began our discussion talking about "Struggle for Peace." He told us that those who seek peace and friendship must first seek a relationship with God. Whenever the relationship with God is joined, the result will be peace and friendship.

He went on to challenge our pacifism and asked if we would not be willing to kill one person in order to save a million. He asked us for examples of situations in which peace came without the use of violence. He concluded our hour of conversation by repeating a verse from the poet Hafez: "If your spirit is pure and you are free of worldly attachments, like Jesus, go to the heavens and from your heart the sun will receive one hundred beams of light." (This poem is included in the chapter "Gifts of Poetry.")

As a tour group we had oil-filled lamps, to which we attached two verses, one from the Bible ("God's word is a lamp to my feet and a light to my path" [Psalm 119:105]) and one from the Quran ("God is the light of the heavens and the earth. God's light may be compared to a niche that enshrines a lamp. The lamp is within a crystal of star-like brilliance" [Quran 24:35]).

A lamp presented to our host in Shiraz.

We presented one of these lamps to our host, which he received with grace and humility. Then he quickly apologized for the fact that he did not have gifts for us.

The next day our bus made an unscheduled stop at his home and each of us was given a wrapped gift, on which was written, "I love you."

This meeting was televised, and the morning newspaper reported on this encounter in a large section. As we boarded an Iranian plane to return from Shiraz to Tehran, we were asked by crew members if we were the peace messengers from North America. As we sat in the plane ready to take off, the pilot gave a warm welcome to the "peace delegation from Canada and America."

Spiritual dialogue. To dialogue together about issues related to our own spiritual journey is perhaps the most important and the most difficult. It is a dialogue in which we reveal vulnerability and ask hard questions about how our beliefs and understandings about God make a difference in how we live our daily lives. We ask questions about how we experience an ongoing, growing relationship with the divine. Spiritual dialogue goes beyond beliefs and theological ideals to the deeper level of the heart, in which our heart is enlarged to know and love God, know ourselves more intimately and love others. It involves seeing ordinary things with the eye of the heart.

As we reflected on our experiences of spiritual dialogue, we were reminded of the farewell words of the fox in the well-known book *The Little Prince* by Antoine de Saint-Exupéry: "And now here is my secret. It is very simple. It is only with the heart that one can see rightly. What is essential is invisible to the eye." Through spiritual dialogue we attempt to gain insight into how it is that we enter the heart in order to see rightly.

Spiritual dialogue is built on a foundation of trust. It was only after many months of building relationships and friendships that we were able to enter this level of dialogue. Reading together the poetry of Iranian poets, especially Hafez, Rumi, and Saadi, was a most significant way of entering spiritual dialogue as these poems reflect the inner dimension of faith and spirituality. This is apparent in the poetry section of this book, which enlarges the topic of spiritual dialogue.

After being in Iran for about a year, one of our Iranian friends was attempting to understand more about the spiritual life of Christians. We had talked earlier about beliefs and practices of both religions. As we conversed, this friend hesitated a moment, looked slightly embarrassed, and then posed a question to me (Evie): "You have watched me pray many times," she began, "but I have never seen you pray. I know you must pray—but how do you pray?"

I was startled to hear her observation and struggled to find words of integrity, not empty phrases. I responded that this has been an area of struggle for me throughout my life. My bookshelf is loaded with books on prayer and how to pray, but it has been only in midlife that I learned a way to pray that was meaningful to me. For me, to pray is to sit in silence as I struggle to lay aside all thoughts and simply open my heart to the presence of God.

This friend seemed very accepting of my response but wondered how often during the day I am obliged to pray in silence. She reminded me of her obligation to pray three times a day. I told her the only obligation I was aware of was the admonition of the apostle Paul to the church at Thessalonica to "pray without ceasing" (1 Thessalonians 5:17).

This response deepened our conversation as this friend then shared that in Islam, one is always to remember God, which, she commented, is like to "pray without ceasing." We laughed when we asked each other, "How does a working woman with a family do that?"

To pray by being silent was an intriguing concept, which we discussed further, and then we realized this could be a significant way for us to pray together: silently sitting together, Muslim and Christian, opening our hearts to the presence of the One, filling the room with peace and joy. Spiritual dialogue occurred during these moments of silent prayer.

Another form of prayer is to remember God. Ways to remember God are built into the very fabric of Iranian daily life. One is always greeted with "salam" ("peace"), to which one is required to respond "salam." When leaving, the appropriate response is "khoda hafez" ("God go with you"). Any activity—eating, traveling, beginning classes or meetings, working on the computer, etc.—must begin with the phrase, "In the name of God the most merciful the most compassionate." It is interesting that when you ask someone, "How are you?" the response is "Alhamdulillah" ("Praise God").

Remembering God by using a string of prayer beads intrigued me. Seeing people walking through the streets, waiting at a bus or taxi stop, riding the bus, sitting in the mosque, or climbing mountains praying with the use of prayer beads made me desirous of learning more about this practice and its meaning.

People were eager to talk with me about the use of prayer beads and reminded me that it was an early practice of Christians as well. I learned that the prayer beads were used to pray and remember the ninety-nine different names for God, which the Quran mentions: the compassionate, the merciful, love, light, all-knowing, etc.

One friend revealed that as she prays the various names for God, she asks herself how these qualities are revealed in her life. Another person related that prayer beads help her remember God by praying three different phrases as her fingers moved about the chain of beads: "God is great," "Thanks be to God," and "Praise God." As a result of these conversations, I decided to make a chain of prayer beads and use them as another way to remember God more constantly. I devised my own words or phrases as I gently held and felt each bead. I kept them in my pocket and prayed as I walked the streets or sat in a park enjoying the flowers and gardens. I used them during periods of loneliness and disappointment to remind myself of the need to trust in God. I used them to remember people who had asked me to pray for them. They helped me feel more connected to the people with whom I was living and sharing life.

We now live near Louisville, Kentucky, not far from where Thomas Merton, the well-known Christian mystic, lived. There is a street in Louisville where Merton received a startling realization. He writes, "In Louisville, on the corner of Fourth and Walnut, in the center of the shopping district, I was suddenly overwhelmed with the realization that I loved all these people, that they were mine and I was theirs, that we could not be alien to one another even though we were total strangers. I have the immense joy of being human, a member of a race in which God became incarnate."[6]

Through our involvement in the dialogue of life, collaboration, theological, and spiritual issues we came to understand Merton's words and felt a deep love for the Iranian people, experiencing them as our brothers and sisters. It is indeed "an immense joy!"

CHAPTER 5

Nightingales and Feather Dusters—Iranian Peacemakers

The opportunity to dialogue with Iranians was a significant peace-building endeavor. As we shared our lives together, collaborated on projects, listened intently, and spoke honestly with one another, seeds of peace were planted. The outcome of such dialogue was a deeper understanding and respect for the other—foundational for building peace.

At the time we were preparing to leave Iran, we discussed with friends and colleagues some of the outcomes of sharing life together as Christians and Muslims. One surprising outcome was the recognition that this experience was personally transformational—we became better Christians and our Iranian friends better Muslims.

As we learned to know and respect the Iranian people, the possibility of a United States military invasion in Iran became unimaginable. Peaceful relations between the United States and Iran were not only our concern but the concern of many of our Iranian friends. Iranians place high value on peace and justice.

The curriculum for our student-exchange program allowed us the option of choosing courses that were of special interest to us. We were eager to learn more about peace and justice from an Islamic perspective, so a special course on peace and Islam was offered. Through this course we had the opportunity to learn about peace from the Quran, *hadiths* (sayings) of the Prophet Muhammad, Persian poets, and important Shia imams of the past.

Teachings about peace from the Quran were a guiding influence for the Shia Iranians. When conversations focused on issues of peace or justice, references to the Quran were often made.

> "True servants of the Merciful are those who walk humbly on the earth and say: 'Peace!' to the ignorant who accost them" (25:63).

> "Let evil be rewarded with like evil. But they who forgive and seek reconciliation shall be rewarded by God. God does not like wrongdoers" (42:40).

> "Take the lead in all good works" (5:48).

We were told that one tradition of the Prophet Muhammad says, "Have I not given you news of something more important than fasting, prayer and alms? It is the removal of hatred and enmity between brothers and making peace between them." The respected Shia Imam Sadiq is known for saying, "The alms that God likes is making peace between people."

Famous Persian poems from Hafez, Rumi, and Saadi contain well-known verses speaking to the importance of peaceful relationships with others. After speaking to a group of students at the University of Kashan, we asked for questions and responses from the students. One student waved her hand vigorously and stated that she had heard we loved Persian poetry. Would we, she asked, repeat a Persian poem to the students in Persian?

There was a sense of excitement and anticipation in the room as the students waited to see our response. Wally began to recite the following verses from the poet Hafez: "Oh friends of generosity and thankful ones of peace, someday be sympathetic to one who has none of this world's goods. The peace of both worlds is in these two words: be kind to your friends, and to your enemies be patient." After speaking the first three words of the poem, the entire room joined in the recitation and finished it with him. Applause and laughter filled the room.

There is a fascinating story in the Islamic tradition about the Old Testament Abraham. According to this story, Abraham had destroyed many idols in the land where he lived, and this action made the people of the land very angry with him. A decision was made to build a huge fire and throw Abraham in.

A blazing fire raged, but the flames were so hot it was impossible to get near enough to throw Abraham in. The solution was to build a catapult, which would launch him into the flames.

Abraham was placed on the catapult and thrown into the burning flames. However, God saved him by sending a flock of nightingales, each with a beak full of water, to fly over the flames and, drop by drop, extinguish it, saving Abraham.

When our Islamic professor shared this story, he expressed his hope for peace in our current world, where raging flames of hatred and misunderstanding fiercely burn. "Could it be," he said, "that the many small actions or tiny 'beakfulls' of peace and justice might quench the daily violence experienced in so many places around the world?"

This insightful question gave us pause as we considered the many "beakfulls" of peace and justice we had experienced in our dialogue and relating with our Iranian friends and in our study of peace in Islam: "small" acts of peace and justice that, drop by drop, help quench the raging fires of misunderstanding, hatred, and violence between the United States and Iran. The following stories illustrate this.

"Salam." When we stepped off the United Arab Emirates' plane and put our feet on Iranian soil for the first time, I (Evie) felt a strange tightening in my stomach, and questions began to swirl in my head: Did we make the right decision to spend the next three years of our lives in a country we had never before visited? Were the people who discouraged us from living in Iran right? Should we really be doing this?

Mehrabad Airport in Tehran looked like none we had ever seen. Women were covered in black chadors, and everyone spoke a language we could not understand. People pushed and shoved to be the first through immigration. I felt ignored as the Iranian passengers ran ahead of us to meet waiting family and friends. Would there be someone waiting for us as well?

We moved with the crowd to be checked by immigration officials. I looked at the different women and men checking visas and passports. Did I want to be in the line where a woman who looked kind and welcoming would check us in? Or, did I want to join the shorter line, which would get me through immigration more quickly?

The shorter line won out as we were eager to get through this first step in living in Iran. I stood behind the red line waiting to step up to the enclosed booth where my credentials for being in Iran would be checked.

"Next!" the immigration officer announced. I moved forward. The officer took my passport and glanced at me through the glass that separated us. "*Salam*," he said. I knew that Persian word well: *peace*. My rapid heartbeat slowed, and I returned the "salam."

I noticed that it took much longer to check my passport and visa than it had another foreign traveler ahead of me. Fear and anxiety began to return since I could understand very little of the questions asked of me.

Great relief came over me as I saw the officer take out the stamp to put in my passport, granting us permission to live in Iran. He handed me back my passport, and without looking at me, said, "Welcome to Iran."

"Salam" was the first word I heard in Iran—a greeting that was exchanged many times each day. When we began our first course on the Quran, our Iranian professor helped us understand its full meaning. "The word salam is related to the word Islam—a religion that brings peace as one surrenders one's soul to God."

Conversations with others begin by offering peace to one another. When a person is addressed with salam, the meaning conveyed is, "You will be safe with me. You will be safe in my mind—that I will think no evil against you; you will be safe in my mouth—that I will speak no unkind words about you; you will be safe in my hands and body—that I will not harm you."

A faithful Muslim knows that when one is greeted with salam, a response in kind is compulsory. In fact the Quran recommends that when greeted with salam, one should reply with an even better greeting (4:86). During times of daily prayers one is forbidden to speak to others. However, if someone greets the person praying with salam, a response is compulsory. When the meanings of this greeting are taken seriously, it is a powerful action to extend and receive the greeting of salam.

Taxis. One of the foundational goals for our living in Iran was to build bridges of understanding and friendship between the American and Iranian people and to help clarify misunderstandings and stereotypes of one another—to be peacemakers. Everywhere we went in Iran, I looked for people and organizations who shared the same goals. Taxi rides turned out to be a journey of such a discovery.

Traveling in Iran can be both easy and difficult. Public transportation is available for any destination and is much easier than driving. There are various options for travel: a bus on which you must wait until it is filled with passengers, a private taxi, or a public taxi (shared with others). We usually chose the bus since it seemed a much safer way to travel. The taxi drivers drive very fast, crossing from lane to lane in cars that may not be air-conditioned or may be quite old. Though our preference was to travel by bus, we soon realized that by traveling in a shared taxi, we would have an opportunity to dialogue with others, an important objective of our being in Iran.

In one such shared taxi we were trying to make our way to a destination in Tehran. Our taxi driver was a college graduate who could not find work in his area of interest so made a living by driving a cab. For the most part he said he enjoyed it but was disappointed not to use his university education to get a job that paid more.

When we got into his taxi cab, he immediately recognized that we were not Iranians and asked where we were from. "I've always wanted to go to the United States," he said, "but have never had the

Evelyn and Wallace Shellenberger

chance. It's a pity our two governments can't work together to allow people to visit. That would help bring peace."

He picked up several other passengers as we continued to weave in and out of the heavy Tehran traffic. It was a Friday, and on occasion after Friday prayers people go out into the streets at the request of their leaders and chant "death to America." On this particular Friday we knew people were marching, for on the cab radio we began hearing the chant we so much disliked.

The taxi driver immediately turned off the radio, turned to us, and said, "I'm so sorry. Our government knows how to unite our people—just find an enemy to rally around." When we stopped at our destination, he asked for no money. "You are guests in our country. Here is my home address and telephone number. The next time you are in Tehran give me a call and we would be pleased to have you come to our home."

Another shared taxi ride provided an unforgettable glimpse of peace. It was a beautiful November morning when we left our Qom apartment to spend the day in Tehran. When we arrived at the taxi terminal, many eager drivers were trying to encourage us to use their services. A seventy-year-old taxi driver somehow managed to get us into his old Peugot, and we patiently waited while he tried to round up two more passengers to ride with us. He was successful when an Iraqi man and a young university student climbed in.

We started on the nearly two-hour trip toward Tehran. The taxi sputtered to a stop several times but thankfully always started again. The university student immediately turned on his MP3 player and rocked to the rhythm of the music. The driver began eating his breakfast of bread and yogurt as he drove and turned on the radio, which filled the cab with Persian love songs.

However, the atmosphere in the cab changed when the Iraqi man, who spoke Arabic and a few Persian and English words, turned to us and in Persian asked where we were from. When we told him we were from the United States, he was silent for a moment and then said he considered us his brother and sister.

The university student sitting next to me (Evie) pulled out his

82

earphones, looked at me, and said, "Are you really from the United States? Are you Muslim? What are you doing in Iran?"

The driver, eager to hear our conversation, turned off the radio.

During the next hour we all became engaged in conversations about our families, the Islamic revolution, the situation in Iraq, and the importance of Christians and Muslims understanding each other better. The conversations were frequently translated into English or Persian, making sure everyone was understood. There were moments when laughter was mingled with deep conversation.

"How old are you?" the university student asked me.

"Sixty-seven," I replied.

"No, you can't be," he replied. "My mother is fifty-five and you look younger than she does." Apparently amazed, he asked the driver how old he thought I was.

The driver looked at me through his rearview mirror and replied, "Eighty-four." The taxi rocked as we all laughed heartily.

When we neared the Tehran terminal, the university student became silent. We all sat in silence for a few moments. The student then sat at the edge of his seat and said, "Think about it; this is pretty amazing. An Iraqi, two very different Iranians, and two Americans have seen each other with the eyes of our hearts, and it has made me very happy."

This experience of "seeing with the eyes of the heart" was indeed amazing—another drop of peacebuilding water on the fires of stereotypes and misunderstandings.

Ramadan. The holy month of Ramadan was my (Evie's) favorite time in Iran. It truly did feel like a holy month as people committed themselves to fasting, prayer, reading the Quran, and giving to the poor. A strong sense of community made itself known during this time. Families gathered each night to share the evening meal—*eftar*—which breaks the day of fasting. I hold fond memories of walking down the streets of Qom during the days of Ramadan, smelling the fragrances of the herbs and spices used to prepare the evening meal, which we were invited to enjoy at many different homes during Ramadan.

During one particular Ramadan, two and a half years after our arrival in Iran, we received an invitation to share an eftar meal on Friday, *jomeh shab*, but with our limited understanding of Persian we mistook the day to be Thursday, *shab-e jomeh*. So that Thursday evening we shared a taxi with our neighbor friends who were also invited to the meal and traveled to the home of our hosts, whom we had met only once before.

We rang the doorbell and waited awhile for the host to answer. I immediately began to wonder if we had come on the wrong day—if we had mistaken Thursday for Friday (a mistake we made often). Soon the host welcomed us into their home, and as is typical in Qom, the women were ushered into one room and the men into another to eat. (This way the women can remove their hijab and eat more comfortably.)

As my friend Heidi and I entered the room where we were to eat, I knew we were not expected guests. However, the hostess quickly welcomed us and hurried to set up the sofreh on the floor. I asked Heidi if we had come on the wrong day. She thought we probably had and went to talk with the hostess, Zainab, about this misunderstanding. Zainab explained that they were expecting us the next day, but a meal could be prepared anyway.

As we talked together, a delicious meal of fish and rice was prepared and laid on the sofreh. Before eating the hostess began laughing, stating that it was one of the easiest eftar meals she had ever prepared. Her good humor made us feel more comfortable. After the meal the food was taken to the kitchen and our conversation continued as we ate fruit and drank tea together.

Zainab recalled a discussion we had shared earlier in which the importance of interfaith dialogue and understanding was stressed. Zainab shared that she had reflected many times on this conversation and had come to realize that she had little opportunity to dialogue with Christians even though she had engaged in serious study about the Christian faith. Zainab's invitation to share a meal together was an attempt to do this and to understand us more personally, particularly as Mennonites.

So Zainab asked me to tell her about Mennonites—who we are and what we believe. I immediately became very anxious, trying to think how I would respond in Persian (it was difficult enough to explain the identity of being Mennonite in English!). I squirmed on my floor pillow, my heart beat rapidly, and I felt a pounding in my chest. *If only I could explain this in English,* I thought. *Where are the Persian words that will help me give a meaningful explanation?*

My friend Heidi noticed my angst, sat forward on her floor pillow, and with passion said she would explain who the Mennonites are. (Heidi had become familiar with the Mennonites through the student-exchange program and was a strong advocate for this program within Iran.) She began by stating that peace and nonviolence are important beliefs, and Jesus's command to "love your enemies" is taken seriously. "For Mennonites, to be followers of Jesus is to live out the words and teachings of Jesus," she said. Heidi discussed with great enthusiasm the relief and development work of MCC in more than sixty countries around the world. "In some countries," she explained, "MCC works side by side with Muslims to care for the poor."

I listened to Heidi's words, spoken so kindly and powerfully about a faith not her own, and I was struck by the enormity of such an act. The experience of a Muslim woman making me known to another, *as I would like to be known,* felt deeply sacred and kind. I wondered, *Would I be able to speak so passionately and kindly about the strengths of her faith?*

As I pondered this, I began to realize that seeds of peace are planted when we can depend on one another to speak respectfully about another's faith and to act as gatekeepers of one another's dignity and pride.

Heidi is an example of an Iranian peacemaker, holding a vision of a new world where God's love reigns supreme, where hospitality to strangers is practiced, and where we outdo one another in showing honor.

Ants. Iranians love gardens, parks, flowers, green spaces, and picnics. Many picnics take place late in the evening or in the morning (for breakfast) when the weather is cool. Families gather; spread a tablecloth on the pavement, desert sands, or parks; and eat and play together.

Our language teacher called early one Friday morning and invited us to join his family at a nearby park for breakfast. We were delighted to get outside and enjoy the company of others. The tablecloth was spread on a concrete slab even though green grass was close by. (We were informed that due to the desert climate it was necessary to protect the grass.)

Enjoying a picnic with our Persian language teacher and his family.

Our breakfast was delicious: warm bread baked on stones from a nearby bakery; fresh Iranian dates from Bam; walnuts, cheese, honey, and whipped cream to put on our bread; and of course tea carried in a huge thermos. Ali, our teacher's two-year-old son, was with us, making us laugh and enjoying our limited Persian.

While we were eating, some ants found their way to our breakfast. When Ali spotted these ants, he jumped up and began swatting them, attempting to chase them away. Ali's father gently took his hand and in typical Persian fashion recited a well-known poem by Persian poet Saadi:

> Don't harm an ant carrying a piece of grain
> because the ant has his own good life.
> Don't oppress the weak and powerless,
> for one day, like the ant, you will be the weaker one.

Ali's father went on to show his son an ant carrying a morsel of bread, and we all marveled as we watched the ants working intently to gather their food. I was in awe at the respect for life taught here to this young boy—respect for the life of the smaller and weaker members of creation. Peacemaking includes peace with all of creation.

Peaceful Protest. During our stay in Iran we experienced the invasion of US forces in Afghanistan and Iraq, neighboring countries to Iran. This provided an opportunity to witness firsthand the effects of the US government's foreign policy on those most directly affected. The weeks and months preceding the US invasion of Iraq were tense times, and the possibility of war was a subject of much discussion with the Iranians.

Iran had been at war with Iraq for nearly eight years during the 1980s, and Saddam Hussein was considered an enemy of the Iranian people. (Many of the Shia Muslims living in Iran had been mistreated under his regime.) We heard many stories from Iranian families about friends and relatives killed in the Iran-Iraq War, and we met people still struggling with the effects of chemical weapons used in this US-supported war. With a history of problems with Iraq, we wondered what the response of the Iranian people would be to a US invasion of Iraq. But in spite of this history, we heard few statements in support of the war. In fact, many Iranians felt deep empathy for the Iraqi civilians, having experienced the effects of war themselves.

Since our Iranian friends knew of our interest in peace and nonviolence, we often were asked how people dedicated to peace respond when war is evident. We responded by sharing stories, letters, petitions, and actions of Americans who were seeking peaceful means to solve the conflict.

One such story concerned former MCC worker Daryl Byler, who, in peaceful protest against the invasion of Iraq, fasted, read scripture, and sent daily letters to government officials pleading for a peaceful resolution. As a result of his fast, women in North America set aside a weekly day of fasting on behalf of the Iraqi people.

I shared this story with a woman friend who was a professor at the University of Qom, and she then shared it with her students, who were touched by the actions of Christians who were fasting for peace and the welfare of their Muslim brothers and sisters in Iraq. As a result, more than twenty-five students decided to join the women in North America for a weekly day of fasting each Friday. They chose to use the Islamic fast, which begins at dawn and ends at dusk. They had been fasting for weeks before I'd been told of their decision to join others. Compassionate, humble peacemakers these students were, breaking boundaries of ethnicity and religion to be part of a movement in support of peace for others.

Return good for evil. Days of disappointment were no strangers to me as I lived in Iran. One significant disappointment occurred when, after spending months planning for an exchange of North American and Iranian women, visas were not granted in time for the exchange to take place. I had great passion for this experience and saw it as a wonderful opportunity for North American women to engage in dialogue and witness the outstanding work of Iranian women throughout the country. This would be an exchange to break down stereotypes on both sides.

When I realized the exchange would not happen, my initial reaction was deep sorrow and anger. I felt a need to take revenge for this personal loss and had thought of what that might be. Fortunately, instead of reacting, I decided to go out into the rainy streets and just walk. I grabbed my prayer beads and a coat to be dropped off at a laundry, if I found one open.

I began my praying: "God be in my mind and in my thinking. God be in my ears and in my hearing. God be in my eyes and in my seeing. God be in my heart and in my loving." This was a prayer I prayed each day before stepping out our apartment door. As I recited this prayer and walked, I gradually began to feel a sense of inner peace and quiet. I accidentally walked beyond the cleaners and quickly turned back to drop off my coat.

The owner of the store greeted me, and I asked if he would be able to clean my coat. Instead of answering, he quickly asked where I was from. I answered, and he then said, "I'm sorry, but I am leaving in about two hours for a New Year's vacation, and my shop will be closed." I thanked him and asked about another place that would be nearby. He gave me directions, and I left to find that place.

After walking nearly a block I heard someone calling, "*Khanom, khanom*" ("Mrs., Mrs."). I turned and the owner of the shop was running to catch up with me. "Come," he said. "I will clean your coat before I go."

I walked back to the shop with him and expressed gratitude that he was willing to do it even though he was getting ready to leave and other clothes were also waiting to be cleaned. He smiled and told me to return in two hours.

When I returned, he was pressing my coat. We talked awhile, and every now and then he would say a word or two in English.

"Do you speak English?" I asked.

He said he was "uneducated" and only learned a few English words in high school. He got his mobile phone and proudly showed me a picture of his eight-year-old son. He told me that he had traveled to Iraq for a spiritual pilgrimage and was captured by the American soldiers and put in prison there for three months.

"Why?" I asked.

He said it was a mistake and that mistakes often happen during wars. He seemed neither angry nor revengeful. "When you told me you were American, I remembered a verse from the Quran that tells us that God loves those who return good for evil, and I wanted to follow the teachings of our holy Quran."

I was touched to be the recipient of such a forgiving act. I took the coat and got out my purse to pay. He told me there was no charge for cleaning the coat—that I was his guest in Iran. I thanked him and handed him the equivalent of several dollars in Iranian rials and asked that he give it to his son as a New Year's gift.

I began walking home, pondering in my heart this unexpected encounter and its meaning for my life. It was the "other," a Muslim, who pointed me back to Jesus's teaching on the importance of forgiving others. When I had failed to see an alternative to revenge, I was given one. The synchronicity of this encounter with my own thoughts of revenge was a gift of great significance. Revenge is not the path to peace; forgiveness is.

Students. During our years of living in Iran we had the privilege of speaking to university students who were studying at various universities throughout the country. Students were intrigued that we, being both Christian and American, had made a choice to live in a Muslim country. These students were interested to know how we experienced Iran, and they also asked to hear stories of what it was like to live in the "West."

Many of these students had never met Americans but had relatives living somewhere in the United States. It seemed to them that life there was "sweet." A topic we were asked to speak about in several universities was the importance of dealing with conflict in peaceful and nonviolent ways.

The first Christmas we were in Iran, a university of fifteen thousand students invited us to its campus to give a lecture on how Christians understand the birth of Jesus. After our acceptance of this invitation, a group of students planned an entire evening to be together with us. When we arrived at the university, we were shocked to see posters hanging throughout the campus announcing our visit and lecture topic.

The students selected a film to begin the evening program. It was *The Song of Bernadette* from 1947, about a teenage girl who had a vision of the Virgin Mary at Lourdes in France. Following the film we were led into a large auditorium where hundreds of students sat and stood to hear what we had to say. A large velvet curtain was drawn on the stage where we were to speak.

Following a piano solo and a recitation from the Quran, the curtain opened, and behind it stood a huge Christmas tree decorated with lights and ornaments. Boxes wrapped in Christmas paper and tied with gold ribbon were under the tree. Sixty large candles burned brightly on the decorated stage. The students applauded as we stood to thank them for this beautiful way of welcoming us to their campus.

Before our presentation, the students were told that they would have an opportunity to write questions on a sheet of paper that would be collected and answered following the lecture. Thirty questions were handed to us after we had spoken. A recurring question had to do with Jesus's teaching that "if someone hits you on the right cheek, you must turn the other also" (Matthew 5:38). Students viewed this commandment as being "weak" and could not understand how turning the other cheek would be a helpful response to a violent act.

The room became quiet as we explained and role-played this teaching of Jesus not as weakness or even deference but as a clever way of turning the tables, to give the oppressor an opportunity for self-reflection. To understand this verse meant understanding the culture of the time and place in which Jesus spoke these words. The students responded with a standing ovation, delighted to have a bit more understanding of a very difficult teaching of Jesus.

As we finished, students flocked around us to learn more about us and the meaning behind our Christmas traditions. We left the university with a stack of e-mail addresses and further questions to be answered via e-mail.

In the weeks following our visit, several students made arrangements to travel to Qom in order to spend more time visiting in our apartment. The commitment of these students to build relationships, to find ways to understand the different other, to ask difficult questions, and to respect and honor differing religious traditions were concrete ways of diminishing the flames of misunderstandings.

Feather dusters. When our three-year assignment in the student-exchange program ended, we wanted to find ways in which other North Americans could experience the people and country of Iran.

"How might our life-changing experience of sharing life with the Iranian people be multiplied?" we asked ourselves.

Through the cooperation of MCC and the institute where we studied, several learning tours were conducted to give others an opportunity to travel through Iran, engage in dialogue, and learn more about Islam. After leading several of these tours through Iran, we asked that members write about their experiences and encouraged them to talk with congressional representatives about what they had experienced in Iran.

**A feather duster being used in Iran as a
means to provide crowd control.**

One tour group member was the peace resource person for MCC Asia. He had traveled throughout Asia working on various peace initiatives. When he completed the tour, he wrote, "Iran is one of the least militarized places I have been in recent years. One does not see guns anywhere, and what might be illustrative as the best of Islamic values, one sees throngs of people being controlled by feather-duster wielding men who gently direct the crowds with colorful red, yellow, and blue household feather dusters. Ya gotta see it to believe it!" Scenes of crowd control in Iran: not tear gas, water blasts, or rifles but soft feather dusters. You do have to see it to really believe it!

Unity Week. When one's eyes are opened to actions of peace among people, it is surprising what is seen and experienced. One such surprise for me was learning about a special week in Iran called "Unity Week." I had been meeting weekly with a friend, Mahnaz, to study the gospel of Luke, and when Mahnaz arrived one afternoon, she explained Unity Week to me.

Apparently the Shia and Sunni Muslims could not agree on the date of the Prophet Muhammad's birth, and they differed by several days on the correct birth date. One of the religious leaders made a recommendation that instead of making this a point of contention, the entire week should simply be called "Unity Week," which would respect the differing viewpoints.

A month earlier I had asked a friend in the United States to buy a Bible for Mahnaz and send it to Iran with the next person traveling there. I received the Bible several days before Unity Week and thought it was an appropriate gift to celebrate our unity in differences.

That Wednesday of Unity Week I had the Bible on the table, eagerly waiting to give it to Mahnaz. When she arrived for our weekly study, she walked in carrying a huge, beautiful bouquet of flowers. The arrangement had been thoughtfully planned. White fragrant flowers called maryam (the name for the mother of Jesus) filled the vase, with a single rose in the center.

"We must celebrate our unity too," she announced, and explained the flower arrangement. Both Christianity and Islam have a deep respect for Mary, the mother of Jesus, so she chose the maryam flower to symbolize that "unity" of respect. The rose honors the One, the divine, in whom all people and all things are united. As I gazed at this beautiful bouquet and smelled its sweet fragrance, I tried to imagine how the concept of Unity Week might be celebrated among groups with opposing and divisive points of view.

Iranians in the United States. In 2009 two Iranian women, a film producer and a university professor, traveled to New York to attend the United Nations conference on women—their first visit to the United States. These women wrote to me ahead of time asking if they could spend a week traveling and visiting organizations devoted to peace and justice. I agreed and, following the UN meetings, met these two Iranian women in Akron, Pennsylvania, to begin a week of traveling together to visit various people and organizations devoted to building peace and justice in the United States and throughout the world.

We began our tour by spending an entire day at the MCC offices in Akron, where these women saw people collecting and preparing to send various material resources to areas of need throughout the world. The director of the peacebuilding program talked about the organization's involvement in confronting racism, violence against women, cluster bomb prevention and removal, and other similar activities.

When we left these offices at the end of the day, both women remarked that it was so important for them to see that there are people in the States working hard for peace in the world. "We mainly see the fighting and wars of the United States," they said.

One topic we discussed while traveling was the separation of church and state in the United States. "How can religion affect society when there is separation?" they wondered. From visits to the MCC Washington office and the Friends Committee for National Legislation, they met staff who told stories of speaking to government officials on various issues of peace and justice and especially on the efforts they are making to promote dialogue with Iran about its nuclear program.

When we walked out of the office around the government buildings in DC, people were carrying posters that read, "Say No to War!" These women were surprised at the freedom to carry such posters around important government places. "I would like some of those posters," one of the women commented. One trip back to the Friends Committee for National Legislation office was all it took to place five such posters in her hands. As we entered Union Station, a well-dressed man approached us and said, "I agree with your posters." She was very surprised at this statement by an unknown person.

Our travels took us to various universities that had peace-building curricula and programs. After several days of experiencing programs and people committed to building peace, both women became reflective and energized thinking about ways to be part of ongoing peace efforts between our two countries. The film producer commented that it was wonderful that they have been able to have this experience. "But," she said, "we are only two Iranians. How can the other people in Iran hear these stories as well?"

Two Iranian women with the faculty and staff at Eastern Mennonite University, Center for Justice and Peacebuilding.

After reflecting a bit on this, she then announced that she must come back with a camera crew and film a documentary. She would interview people working for peace and also spend a week in an American home to show how families live here. Her stereotypes of Americans and family life had been challenged, and she wanted to correct misunderstandings of her people in Iran.

Through the light of their candles, perhaps a more balanced picture of the American people might be possible in Iran. The work of promoting peace between Iran and the United States, between Muslims and Christians is ongoing. We continue to have hope that feather dusters will replace instruments of violence and that small efforts of peace, like small drops of waters in the nightingales' beaks, will cool the burning flames of misunderstanding and hatred.

———— C H A P T E R 6 ————

Covered Heads—Uncovered Stereotypes

A topic of great interest and concern for the audiences to whom we spoke upon our return from Iran was the status of women in Iran. In most of these settings we engaged this topic by asking audiences to think of words or phrases that come to mind when picturing a woman from Iran. The responses in nearly every audience were similar: oppressed, forced to cover themselves, subjected to the demands of men, a slave to her spouse, not equal to men, isolated, sad, and works primarily in the home.

These responses reflect stereotypes of Iranian women common to our Western minds. These generalizations may create social distance between cultures and limit true understanding and empathy. "Stereotyping robs individuals and groups of complexity, reducing them to the crude dimensions of a 'type.' This is

Veiled woman by Rachel Friesen, former student at Goshen College, Goshen, Indiana.

particularly destructive when the individual or group has a history of being defined in narrow or negative ways by the dominant group."[7]

Western stereotypes tend to picture Iranian women as those to be pitied and "rescued." Although the current Iranian government has, in some ways, been repressive and oppressive toward women, many Iranian women would say that *Western* ideas of the role of women in society are not the answer for them. Iranian women carry a strong sense of pride and optimism that they can deal with issues about women in their own unique ways. And they are!

Stereotypes about Iranian women often arise due to images of their being covered or veiled. This veiling is referred to in Iran as hijab, or chador. The literal translation of chador in Persian is "tent." Basically, the chador is a semicircular piece of cloth, often black, wrapped around the body and head, and gathered at the chin. The chador is worn by women throughout Iran, though many women choose to wear slacks with a more modified covering consisting of a head scarf and a loose tunic or coat known as a mantow. Although the type of hijab may vary, covering the head and body (except the face and hands) is a requirement for all women in Iran, including visitors.

Evie with Iranian friends in Qom.

After the Islamic Revolution in 1979, wearing the chador became a symbol of resistance against the previous Pahlavi regime and Western values endorsed by the regime. A diverse group of women across class and society chose to wear the chador at that time. Years later, however, it was not uncommon to hear women resist the imposition of dress by the government. The initial expectations of an Islamic government were not realized for some women, and they reacted to this disappointment by refusing to wear the chador. As one travels throughout Iran, a diverse variety of hijab is apparent.

**A group of young Iranians at the tomb of
the famous Persian poet Saadi.**

Some women feel it is their responsibility to support the dress codes imposed by the government and would monitor women's dress by confronting those who did not meet its standards.

One Friday morning I was invited to attend a demonstration following Friday prayers. As I stood at the march among the crowd, an older woman approached me and began to scold me for the fact that some of my hair was showing, which she said was disrespectful. A Muslim cleric, standing near me, stepped in front of the woman, asked her to stop, and reminded her that her behavior was disrespectful, since I was a guest in Iran. This brought me a sense of peace.

An Iranian engineer.

I left the march puzzled at what I experienced. How could this Iranian woman scold me about the small amount of hair showing from my covering? Had she any idea how challenging this dress code was for me, how insulating it felt? As I thought about it more, I realized that my visible hair represented the differing views of Iranian women regarding Islamic dress code for women—some more conservative, some more liberal. And as illustrated here, Iranian women are not shy about expressing their own particular point of view. (I also witnessed this determination to speak one's viewpoint at security checks in Iranian airports where older women would sometimes stop younger women wearing fingernail polish or makeup and require them to take it off before boarding the plane.)

Though expressed differences and understandings regarding dress and hijab were apparent among Iranian women, other aspects of women's roles in society are supported by most women. Education for girls and women, for example, is highly valued. In fact, in most universities throughout Iran, more than half of the student body consists of women.

Women attending universities enroll in all major fields of study, with engineering ranking among the highest. While traveling throughout Iran it was no surprise to see women employed in many different professional roles: bankers, professors, physicians, researchers, parliament members, engineers, taxi drivers, and executive directors of large nonprofit and government organizations.

Personal stories of Iranian women. The personal lives and stories of Iranian women are as diverse as the women themselves. By entering their stories one can get a glimpse of their world. The following stories will introduce you to several Iranian women, their way of life, and their views about important issues. All of the women are personal friends and may not be identified by their real names.

Narjes. Narjes studied Persian literature at the university and currently serves as a professor of Persian literature and English (speaking and teaching English) at a university in Iran. She is deeply spiritual, committed to Islam, and open and conversant about other faith traditions. Narjes has traveled outside Iran numerous times as a tourist or a conference speaker or participant. Writing, research, and translations of texts from English to Persian are part of her personal resume.

Given Narjes's "liberal" resume and professional work, I was surprised to realize that Narjes also is deeply committed to wearing a chador, allowing only her face and hands to be seen. Wondering if she felt obligated to do so, I asked her about this, and she was eager to tell me her story:

Before the Iranian Revolution in 1979, women were required by the Shah to remove their scarves and chador. Prior to that time, as she was reading the Quran and contemplating this issue, she came to believe that wearing the chador was the right thing for her to do no matter what the political dictates might be. She recalls feeling a deep sense of peace when she came to this decision—a sense of peace that has continued to this day. "Wearing hijab is currently an obligation of the government, but I would wear it even if it were not," she said. "My inner convictions dictate my actions."

Narjes spoke about a sense of freedom in wearing the chador and stated that wearing it helps focus on inner rather than outer beauty. Narjes believes her physical beauty is reserved primarily for the eyes of her husband.

Late one afternoon I visited Narjes. She greeted me wearing a lovely dress, gold jewelry, and beautifully styled hair. "Oh, Narjes," I said, "you must be going somewhere since you are all dressed up."

She laughed and replied, "No, my husband will be coming home soon, and I wanted to look nice."

I couldn't help but think of the difference between us. Did I ever dress up because my husband would be coming home? No. But it did make me think about it.

Narjes taught me cultural expectations and norms in Iran, and it was in her home that I learned the secrets of cooking various Persian meals. Narjes lives a life of hospitality and invited us weekly to share a meal in her home and to spend holidays with her extended family. She taught me how to shop in unfamiliar markets and stores and cautioned me that as a foreigner I may be asked to pay higher prices than Iranians.

**Enjoying an Iranian meal with Narjes's extended
family seated around the sofreh.**

On one specific occasion, after I had been out of the country for several months, I visited a neighborhood grocery store and told the grocer I wanted to buy a chicken. I knew food prices had increased since I had been gone, but when the grocer stated the price for the chicken, I was shocked. I expressed my shock and tried to bargain, but the grocer insisted that this was the current price.

Afterward, I dropped off the chicken at our apartment and walked to Narjes's home to inquire about the price of chickens. Needless to say, Narjes was outraged at the price I had paid and asked that I accompany her to the store so she could confront the grocer about this "injustice."

We walked together, and Narjes's determination to confront this was seen clearly in her resolute and determined walk. I, on the other hand, felt a bit timid and unsure whether I wanted to be part of this. I told Narjes that it may be better for me to learn this lesson without the confrontation. She quickly replied, "No! This is not the way Muslims are to do business."

We entered the store, and the grocer looked startled to see Narjes with me. She minced no words in telling him that he had cheated me in selling the chicken at such a high price. She reminded him that this went against Islamic beliefs and because of this, she would never buy meat at his store again. He offered to make it right by giving me another chicken for free.

As we returned home, Narjes expressed her disappointment when Islamic values are not lived out. Narjes continues to be an advocate for justice. She is determined to confront injustice wherever and whenever it occurs, as she did in this particular situation.

On one particular occasion, we journeyed together from Canada to the United States. Narjes commented that she did not look forward to the time when we would have to cross the border between Canada and the United States. She knew that being an Iranian citizen might lead to long periods of questioning by immigration personnel.

Many miles before we were to reach the US border, Narjes pulled a small book from her purse and quietly read in the backseat. After a while I asked what she was reading. She commented that it was a prayer book; she wanted to pray that our passage to the United States would be peaceful. She spoke no more until we crossed the border. She then put her prayer book away, smiled, and said, "Thanks be to God."

Narjes lived an active professional and family life. She modeled a life of deep faith, evident in words and actions. Her faith was important in decisions she made for her own life, but she was never judgmental about others who chose differently.

Zainat. When I first met Zainat, she was in her early twenties, had completed her university education, and was determined to get a PhD in engineering in the United States.

Zainat grew up in a large family of modest income that could afford only the basic necessities. She remembers sleeping on the floor in the hall so her elderly ailing grandmother could have a room. (Families in Iran claim the responsibility to care for the older generation; placement in a nursing facility is usually not an option.)

No one in Zainat's family was a university graduate, and she was determined to be the first. She studied hard. Most of her studying occurred late at night when others were sleeping, due to the noise at home during the day. Zainat knew that acceptance into a university in Iran would be difficult, and in order to be accepted, she must pass the Iranian University Entrance Exam, known as *concours*.

The competition for admittance is fierce—only 10 percent of all applicants are admitted to the many universities. More than a million students take the exam, Zainat explained to me, and of those, only about 150,000 are accepted. But Zainat's hard study paid off when she passed the exam and was accepted into a university.

With a college diploma in hand, Zainat was now ready to pursue a PhD program. To gain acceptance into a graduate program in the United States meant dedication and perseverance. She enrolled in an English-learning program to become fluent in English; researched all the engineering programs available to her and the requirements for admission; saved money to pay the necessary expenses to get to the United States and enroll in a PhD program; and researched visa requirements and procedures to obtain a student visa. Zainat told no one, except one sister, of her plans to leave Iran to study abroad. Her family would be informed once the visa was approved.

In 2010 Zainat's hard work paid off, and she was admitted to an engineering program in the United States. She is currently completing this program. Talking about her doctoral dissertation excites Zainat, and we witnessed this excitement as we listened to her explain her research, which has to do with developing methods to reinforce concrete in order to withstand the force of blasts.

Zainat is the only women in the engineering department at her graduate school working on this project, but she finds great support from her professors and advisors. She is now wondering how to use her skills in obtaining a career.

In Iran, Zainat wore a chador when outside the home. She has chosen not to wear hijab in the United States. When I asked her about this change, she said she never believed the hijab was necessary: "Allah cares about what is in our heart, not what is on our head." She continued, "Wearing hijab should be a choice that one makes, not something that is dictated. I have deep respect for Muslim women who choose to cover their heads and deep respect for those who do not." For Zainat, the actions and behavior of people toward others speak about the importance of faith much more than clothing and coverings.

Zainat represents traits I have seen in so many Iranian women: commitment to education, high goals for a professional life, perseverance in the midst of extreme difficulties, courage, and a faith deeply rooted not in doctrine and rules but in love, compassion, and mercy.

Fatimeh. In Shia Islam, a temporary marriage, known as *sigheh*, is permitted. During the Iran-Iraq War (1980–88) many Iranian men were killed, leaving thousands of widows. It was at this time that the government promoted temporary marriages or polygamy to deal with the economic burdens of the war and also the moral dilemma of having so many unmarried women. In the first decade of the twenty-first century, temporary marriages were still practiced.

In this kind of marriage the man and woman agree on and commit to a specific duration and compensation of the marriage. The duration of the marriage can be for several hours or for many years. Any child born from this union is provided for financially by the father and is able to inherit property or money following the death of the father. The marriage is understood to be temporary and differs from a permanent marriage, which is meant to be a lifelong commitment.

I was introduced to Fatimeh by her husband, a student at one of the Iranian universities. She was forty years old and did not have a secondary education. She lived with her "temporary" husband in a small, simple home. In preparation for our visit she prepared a delicious Persian meal of saffron rice and a chicken-based stew. A number of times she apologized for not preparing more food. Following the meal, we sat together on the floor, enjoying fresh fruit and tea. She told me her story without embarrassment.

Fatimeh was previously married and had birthed several children. Fatimeh's husband soon became involved in the use of addictive drugs and abusive behavior. She knew that a divorce would mean that her children would be given to their father, but she could no longer live in such an abusive relationship. She also knew that as a divorced woman, her chances of living in a lifelong, permanent marriage in Iran were very slim.

Eventually, Fatimeh obtained a divorce, through which her husband was granted custody. Fatimeh said she deeply missed her children and would secretly travel to the city where they lived, find a hiding place close to the home, and watch for the children. Tears filled her eyes as she talked about each of the children. She expressed anger about the legal system in Iran that would allow an addicted and abusive father to have guardianship, a legal system favoring the rights of men.

As a single woman it was difficult to find a job and financially support herself. "My life changed for the better when I met Ali, and we agreed to have a temporary marriage," she said. Ali was able to support Fatimeh financially and help her buy the equipment necessary to set up a small business in their home. She acknowledged the temporary nature of the marriage and understood that a permanent marriage at this point was not possible. "I am grateful for the opportunities this marriage has given me," she stated. "I have now experienced a relationship with another man that has not been abusive, and I am now able to support myself when our marriage ends."

Fatimeh felt a new sense of self-confidence in being able to provide income that could sustain her when the marriage ended.

I asked Fatimeh if she had met her husband's family, and she said they did not know their son was living in a temporary marriage. She informed me that it would hinder his chances of marrying a permanent wife. Fatimeh agreed to a temporary marriage at a time when she was alone, unable to find employment, and financially desperate. Though she had appreciated the benefits of her temporary marriage, she also told of continuing periods of depression, not knowing when she would once again be on her own.

Fatimeh shared her story with honesty and vulnerability She expressed pain, depression, and gratitude, as well as anger toward an unjust legal system that granted parenting rights to an addicted and abusive man. She supports those women in Iran who are actively working to see that family laws are changed to provide more equality for women. Compared to her earlier life, a temporary marriage had given her self-confidence and an opportunity to learn new skills, which would help ensure an independent financial future.

Maryam. Taxis are the preferred way to travel in the busy capital city of Tehran, and so I was delighted one particular day to have as my taxi driver Maryam from the Ladies' Wireless Taxi Service. When I entered Maryam's taxi (the back of which read "www.womentaxi. IR"), I expressed my appreciation for the availability of a taxi service dedicated to serving only women.

Maryam informed me that more than sixty thousand women use taxi services each day in Tehran, and much excitement had mounted around forming a taxi service run by women for women. There are many women drivers in Iran, but a taxi service owned and run by women is a new thing, not only in Iran but in most other countries. Maryam recognized that in most countries, driving taxis is a male-dominated occupation, and Iranian women are at the forefront in forming a taxi business.

Maryam talked freely and said her job had given her many opportunities to meet people and develop new friendships. She took pride in the initiative taken by women to develop services that relate to the needs of women. Driving a taxi involves a lot of training to prepare for all the possible situations in which a taxi driver might find herself. I asked Maryam if she had experienced any negative responses to the all-women taxi service. "I'm sure there are some," she said, "but all my customers have been happy to ride with us."

Maryam is an example of other Iranian women breaking gender stereotypes and taking pride in the achievements of women within her country. The development of this organization demonstrates that Iranian women have been able to make important gains in a political system that tends to keeps women subordinate to men. Maryam is also one of thousands of young women in Iran who support a grassroots movement, known as "One Million Signatures

Campaign," or "Campaign for Equality," working for more equality between men and women.

Zainab. When we met Zainab, she was twenty-six years old and was planning a wedding, which we had been invited to attend. Zainab was marrying a man she met while attending university, and though not an arranged marriage, both parents agreed to it. She would be an *aqdi* wife in a marriage that was intended to be permanent. Zainab had gotten to know her future husband well while attending university with him. They had talked about their future, and both expected to find employment outside the home.

Zainab said she and her future husband would sign a contract for their marriage, which would define the expectations for each one. "The marriage contract is different for each couple," she stated, "and may state any requirement important either for the husband or wife."

"Would you share what will be written in your marriage contract?" I asked.

Zainab told me that the statements of the marriage contract were an important topic between her and her fiancé. The marriage contract would ask for fourteen gold coins as a bride-price, or *mehriye*. The number fourteen was important to her as the number represented the twelve Shia imams, and Imam Ali (the son-in-law of the Prophet Muhammad), and Fatimeh, the prophet's daughter. An approximate value of these coins would be six thousand dollars. These gold coins would be paid to her by her husband upon her demand, which she said would be only if they would divorce. Zainab said the contract would require her husband to give her one-half of all the assets if he chose to divorce her. Although polygamy is very uncommon in Iran, the marriage contract would forbid Zainab's husband to take a second wife without her permission.

Zainab liked the concept of a marriage contract because it spelled out some important expectations for the marriage. However, Zainab's hope was for love, understanding, and an equal sharing of marriage responsibilities, all of which are not explicitly stated in a marriage contract.

Another important conversation Zainab shared with her fiancé before their marriage was about children—how many they wished to have and when they would be ready to parent them. Zainab shared that Iran had a very thorough educational program on family planning, and all couples wishing to be married were required to take classes on birth control and planning for children—classes that covered many topics: the male and female reproductive system, sexual intercourse, methods of contraception and the necessity to use birth control, and the advantages of small families. Contraceptives were offered free to married couples and could be easily acquired.

Zainab emphasized that being spiritually and emotionally ready to have children was important. "All children must be wanted and planned for," she said. For many married couples, two children is the norm.

Zainab also talked about the difficulties young people face in Iran when they want to get married. "It is very expensive to get married here," she commented, "and I am one of the lucky ones to have enough money to buy all the things we need to be married."

As a new wife she would be expected to purchase all the necessary appliances and furnishings for their new apartment. With the help of her family, Zainab had nearly everything she would need to start her own home.

Once married, Zainab's husband would be financially responsible for the economic needs of the family. She said, "After our marriage, the money I make in my job is basically mine, to use as I desire. Of course I want to help out with our expenses, but I am not required to do that in Islam." She went on to explain that in Islam, a mother can request payment from her husband for breastfeeding and providing care for the children. "I wouldn't do that," she continued, "but I think it places value on the role of the mother in the home."

The time for Zainab's wedding came while we still were living in Iran, and we enjoyed the experience of participating as guests in an Iranian wedding. As in most cultures, weddings in Iran are occasions for joy and celebration.

Two different parts of a marriage celebration may occur on the same day or weeks later.

The first part of the celebration is called *aghd,* meaning "knot." In this ceremony, both parties and a chosen witness for each sign the agreed-upon marriage contract in the presence of family and close friends. Normally this ceremony takes place in the home of the bride, which usually is decorated with flowers and a special *sofreh-e aghd* (tablecloth).

On Zainab's sofreh-e aghd, many special items were placed: flowers, the Quran, special nuts and sweets, a mirror, and two candle stands. Zainab dressed in a Western-style wedding dress and veil and sat with her husband under a silk cloth held by two female relatives. Zainab's fiancé was asked if he wished to enter into the marriage contract, and she was then asked the same question. When Zainab was asked, she paused and remained silent. The question was repeated three times, and after the third time she responded with yes. Zainab explained that this tradition makes the bridegroom wait for the bride's answer, showing that her consent is very important to him.

Following the signing of the marriage contract, two sugar cubes were rubbed together above the cloth covering the bride and groom, as a symbolic act to sweeten the couple's married life. Feasting on delicious Persian foods and sweets followed the official wedding traditions.

The second part of Zainab's wedding celebration occurred several months later when more than five hundred relatives and friends gathered to feast and celebrate the new marriage. Laughter and conversation during this celebration continued for hours—in the absence of any alcohol!

Farideh. We first met Farideh when she accompanied one of the learning tour groups through a museum in Iran. She eagerly greeted our tour group and warmly welcomed us to the museum. Her English language skills were excellent, and as she led us around the museum, telling us about ancient artifacts, she also engaged us in conversations about life in Iran and life in the United States.

Farideh was a young mother of one daughter and a university graduate. She grew up in Tehran and enjoyed the many opportunities the city provided her. Many Fridays she would hike into the mountains with a group of hikers to enjoy the gifts of nature. In the season of winter she enjoyed skiing in the Alborz Mountains north of Tehran. Her face glowed as she shared her joy of the outdoors. She said that tourists often acted surprised when she talked about the many sports and physical activities that Iranian women engage in. Many women go to the parks on a regular basis to run and exercise. "Why is it," she asked, "that this aspect of our lives as Iranian women surprises you?" Perhaps the answer lies in some of our long-held stereotypes of Iranian women: "isolated, sad, confined to the home."

A group of Iranian youth enjoying the beautiful mountains in Iran.

Pride and joy were palpable as she talked about her eight-year-old daughter, who was a good student and enjoyed accompanying Farideh into the mountains. Farideh talked about the difficulty she was experiencing in balancing work, family life, and the need for personal recreation. She wondered how women in the United States and Canada balance work and family expectations. As a response our common women-hearts began beating as one when we shared together about this reality that touches many women, regardless of nationality or religion.

Farideh was asked by one of the tour group members how she experienced wearing the required hijab. She responded by saying she believed the decision to wear hijab should be a personal one and not dictated by the government. She added that she felt sorrow for her young daughter who only saw veiled women in public. Farideh anticipated the day in Iran when she could live out her personal convictions regarding hijab. She not only anticipates that day but is finding ways of working together with other women to promote freedom of choice for women.

Reflections from tourists to Iran. Following our student-exchange program, Wally and I had the privilege of leading North American learning tours in Iran to experience Iran and the women living in Iran in particular. Many stories followed this experience, stories that add a varied perspective on Iranian women. Among the stories were these:

From a Canadian woman: "We entered a teahouse that was, of all surprises, full of teenage girls. They all chimed out, 'Hello! Welcome to Iran!' After talking with us for a while, these Iranian teenagers started snapping photos and positioned us—North American women—next to them with arms entwined, like we were best friends. When our Iranian host told the girls we needed to leave, one young girl walked up to the robed professor and told him firmly that he was not to take us away until she had taken a photo of us with her, and that was final. The professor backed down. Contrary to another stereotype, neither the chador nor Islam had made any of these young women submissive."

From another Canadian woman: "Here in Iran I met so many happy, spontaneous young women with bright dreams and goals— women who felt empowered, confident, and determined to get their PhDs among other things. The women in our touring group visited an impressive Islamic seminary for women in the city of Qom. Women from all over Iran and the world came here to receive a high-quality education. We also met a young Californian woman who came to this seminary to study for a year but ended up extending her studies to four years. I'm not surprised. It is a beautiful, spacious campus with covered walkways, blue tiles, pointed arches, fountains, pools, and gardens, all of which created a sense of peace and spirituality. As I watched the chattering girls move past to their next class, looking like robed Oxford academics, I couldn't help but think how lucky they were that they didn't have to deal with the destructive pressures that our Canadian high schools put on our young women: the pressure to look cool, to experiment with drugs and sex, and to rebel—to become someone they are not. I also was suddenly aware of how wonderful it was to be free of all the sexual exploitation of women in advertising."

A man from the United States said, "One of my enduring images of Iran is the Iranian woman wearing the chador. For the West, the chador is a symbol of draconian and oppressive religious domination of women. But what we [tourists] heard and experienced were stories of how much more freedom women now have than they did before 1979 when the Shah was in power. What we saw were women in parliament, women driving cars, women working in all professional fields. Women themselves spoke of a freedom from the oppressive style and crazed expectations of the Western fashion world by wearing the simple black covering. This is not to deny the frustration of the women in our tour group [non-Muslims] who had to cover when in public and wear a scarf and coat in the extreme summer heat."

A heartfelt tribute to Iranian women. It has been a deep privilege to experience the friendship of many different Iranian women. They have been friends, teachers, soul mates, and sisters. I walked as a pilgrim among a people and land I did not know. Iranian women gave me welcome in their homes and invitations to hear and share stories of our common humanity. These strangers became my sisters. They have renewed my sense of hope for peace between our nations and religions. The words of a dear friend, Mahnaz, reveal truth: "The seedbed of hatred is ignorance of the other; the seedbed of love is knowledge of the other."

CHAPTER 7

Gifts of Poetry[8]

For our Iranian friends, reciting Persian poetry, especially the poetry of Hafez (1325–89), is like second nature. Most of them have memorized many poems and are always ready to recite a verse or several verses to emphasize a point of discussion. While we were living in Iran, our friends would often share entire poems with us, and this sharing became an important part of our relationships. Once we had learned enough Persian to be able to decipher a poem, we wouldn't usually understand it right away, so we would keep the poem in our pockets and take it out to discuss the meaning with our Iranian friends. This sharing gave life to our conversations.

In much of classical Persian poetry, the link between verses is not obvious to a non-Persian reader and therefore may seem disjointed and choppy. However, for the Persian reader, the verses are linked by similar-sounding words, particularly verbs, and by rhythm. The poem, as a whole, is unified by addressing a specific human experience. At the end of a poem, the poet will often offer an insightful comment about himself.

Beauty and love are recurring themes in Persian poetry, especially in relation to the divine. Divine beauty is one of the themes these poetic metaphors: a woman's beauty, a graceful cypress, and a rose, refer. Divine beauty is, paradoxically, inviting and evasive, revealing and disguising, liberating and binding, illuminating and obscuring. Divine beauty can evoke love, but the beloved (the divine) usually does not meet the expectations of the lover, which results in grief. Love first warms the heart and then heats the heart through disappointment. The fire of grief burns away the armor of the "self" or the "I" to make room for the beloved, the divine.

Two other recurring metaphors in Persian poetry include the nightingale, representing the lover, and wine, representing love. Intoxication with wine is a metaphor for extravagant love. The one who sells or brings the wine can function as a metaphor for the divine, a divine messenger, or a human spiritual guide.

In addition to these metaphors, Hafez uses the Sufi, wearing the woolen coat, to represent one who projects an outward display of piety. He uses an ascetic to represent one whose good deeds and worship are for the benefits of heaven's reward.

The Persian word *rendi* is important in Hafez's poetry. It carries the meaning of an extravagant experience of and response to God's love, which lacks inhibition and is not limited by social and religious expectations. The experience of God's love is like being intoxicated, or like "the sinful woman" of the gospels who pours costly perfume on Jesus's feet and then wipes them with her hair.

A final element of the Persian language to take note of is that the same word serves as pronoun for masculine, feminine, and neuter. In other words the same pronoun can indicate the feminine, the masculine, and the inanimate metaphors referring to the divine. This makes for interesting reading of some passages.

Arriving at an understanding of a Persian mystical poem is like mining for sapphires. When we first read the poem, it carries no meaning; we don't even understand the words. After consulting various dictionaries, commentaries, and another translation, we can begin to link the words into units of thought. We can gradually read the poem, but it continues to feel and sound awkward and disjointed. As we read it over and over again, more and more quickly, and with the right rhythm, the poem begins to coalesce, and the meaning becomes a bit clearer. We then read the poem again with our Iranian friends and discuss its meaning. After (or perhaps *through*) many hours of language work and conversation, the poem reveals its beauty and cohesion, and we find ourselves wrapped in a sense of peace and calm. Only then can our translation of the poem begin.

The following poem is one of many that demonstrate the end result:

"The Friends Beauty Is Enough for Us"

گلعذاري ز گلستان جهان ما را بس

In the rose garden of the world
the one with rosy cheeks
is enough for us.
Of the soft green meadows,
the shadow of the swaying cypress
is enough for us.

Alas, I am part of humanity
seeking fortune and fame,
but really, of all the world's riches
a cup of rich wine
is enough for us.

A castle in heaven will be given
as a gift for good deeds.
We are misfits.[9] Begging
at the tavern door
is enough for us.

Sit by the side of a stream
and watch your lifetime pass.
This sign of the world's passing
is enough for us.

Consider the wealth and pain of this world.
If you do not learn from this,
know this profit and loss
is enough for us.

We have the friend with us;
what more could we want?
The value of this soul friend
is enough for us.

O God, do not send us from your door
to the delights of heaven,
for of all this world can offer,
to be on your sidewalk
is enough for us.

O Hafez, your nature
is to complain of injustice.
But like a spring of water,
you and your flowing poems
are enough for us.
—Ghazal of Hafez 268[10]

It is said that almost every Iranian Muslim household has a copy of the Quran and a copy of Hafez's poetry. We heard from many Iranians that Hafez and Rumi are the interpreters of the spiritual meaning of the Quran. After we had finished reading through the Quran with the help of an Islamic scholar, we then were encouraged to read the poetry of Hafez. Most of the poems that follow are part of the collection of the *ghazals* (poems) of Hafez. These poems do not bear titles, nor are they arranged by theme or subject; rather, they are organized alphabetically by the last letters of the first *hemistitch* (half-line) of the poem. In the selection of poems below we have given each poem a title from a word or phrase that occurs in the first line of the poem; the title is then followed by the first hemistitch in Persian script.

The first seven of these poems were introduced to us by one of our professors well-versed in the poetry of Hafez, and the remainder of the poems by other friends. Our professor is tall, thin, quiet, and very gentle. While we walked with him in the garden of the university where he teaches, he spoke softly to the gardeners. The gardeners would respectfully greet him with, "I look up to you," and he would receive these greetings with great humility.

While we sat on a bench among the birds singing in the trees, he told us about which tree in Iran produces the best walnuts and where to buy the best dates, but most of all he talked about the poetry of Hafez. Wally spent about forty hours with him as he helped us read and understand the ghazals of Hafez and their relationships to the Quran. This dear friend of ours introduced us to the following poem and to the next six ghazals. Following some of the poems in this selection, Wally has provided brief "paraphrases" to facilitate the reading.

"The Garden Youths"

رونق عهد شبابست دگر بستان را

The freshness of youthful vigor
is replayed in the garden;
the sweetly singing nightingale
bringing good news to the rose.

O, morning breeze,
if you meet these garden youths,
take our greeting to them:
the basil, cypress, and rose.

If the young wine seller appears,
with my eyelashes
I will sweep the threshold
of her tavern door.

O, you whose face
is ringed with dark fragrant curls,
take it easy;
I am dazzled.

I'm afraid for those who laugh
at the veterans drinking this wine—
that the tumult of *their* first drink
will destroy their faith.

Be like Noah,
a humble man of God
who feared the typhoon
no more than a drop of water.

Leave this world,
do not seek its delights and treasures.
For this jealous bowl, in the end,
brings death to its guests.

Each person in their last resting place
is a fistful of dust.
What use is it
to build mansions to the sky?

My soul, you have a throne
in the kingdom of God[11]
when you bid good-bye
to this world's prison.

O Hafez, drink wine, enjoy yourself,
be extravagant in love,[12]
but don't, as others,
get caught acting against the Quran.
~Ghazal 9

Paraphrase summary of Ghazal 9:

The experience of God's beauty and love
is invigorating;

it is captivating.
Take care!
For the following tumult
can shake your faith.
Be like Noah,
who did not fear the storm!
Set aside self
so it does not stand in the way
of receiving God's love!

✹

"Our Heart's Desire"
ساقي بنور باده برافروز جام ما

By the light of your wine,
kindle our hearts.
Sing out, "Our heart's desire
has been fulfilled!"

O you inexperienced in the joy
of always drinking this wine,
we have seen in the cup's reflection
the face of the friend.

The person whose heart is enlivened by love
will never die.
Our endurance is recorded
in the news of the universe.

How many were the
winks and nods of this world,
when our swaying cypress came,
moving with splendor and grace.

O wind, if you pass the garden
of those lovers,
be sure to give the
dear friends our message.

Say, "Why are you trying to forget our name?
It is of no use!
For our name will come to you
by the power of our name alone."

Intoxication is good in the eyes
of the one who holds our hearts.
Therefore the reins of our control have
been given into the hands of intoxicating love.

I suspect that on judgment day
the sanctioned bread
will have less value than
our forbidden wine.

Hafez, from your eyes,
scatter grains of longing tears.
Perhaps the dove of union
can be lured into our trap.

There is the deep-blue sea
of God's heaven and we,
the ship of the crescent moon,
are submerging into God's boundless love.[13]
~Ghazal 11

Paraphrase summary of Ghazal 11:

The love of the beloved
brings life, joy,
and permanence.

However, there are
competing loyalties;
still, the beloved
keeps coming.

In the end our heart
is satisfied in the
intoxication of,
the union with,
being submerged in
God's love.

❋

"The Way of the Heart"
برو بکار خود، اي واعظ، این چه فریادست

O you and your preaching!
What are you saying?
Stick to your own affairs!
I've left the way of piety;
I'm on the path of the heart;
what about you?

He is created by God
yet he has not solved
even a tiny problem
of his own existence.

As long as I can't, like a flute,
touch the beloved's lip,
all the advice in the world
is wind in my ear.

Beggars at your door
have no need of eight heavens.
They are prisoners of your love
and of both worlds they are free.

Even though this love intoxication
destroys me,
my essence will emerge
from the ruins, blooming.

O heart, don't complain
of the friend's injustice,
for the oppression of the beloved
is in fact justice.

O Hafez, are you trying to reassure me?
Well don't.
I have had my fill
of reassurances.
~Ghazal 35

Paraphrase of Ghazal 35:

I've stopped preaching;
it does not solve a problem.
I'm now on the path of love;
I long for the beloved.
As a prisoner of your love
I've no need of heaven.
My love of the friend
has ruined self-centering.
I complain, but really
it is a kindness.
Hafez, don't reassure;
I've had my fill of that.

"Strangers Are Waiting"

روی تو کس ندید و هزارت رقیب هست

No one has seen your face
yet a crowd of strangers is waiting.
There is the bud, and for you,
a hundred nightingales are singing.

When I come to your dwelling
is it not strange,
that, like me, there are
thousands of strangers?

In the realm of love,
of the Sufi lodge or the tavern[14]
there is no difference!
For in every place
the beloved's face is radiant.

Where deeds of the
monastery can be seen,
is also the peal of the bell
and the sign of the cross.

What about the lover, whose
beloved pays no attention?
O, friend, what's the problem?
Is there pain? There is the physician!

The lament of Hafez
is no idle tale!
It is a strange story
and also astonishing!
~Ghazal 63

Paraphrase of Ghazal 63:

Thousands of us
are waiting for you.
Piety and extravagance;
you are comfortable with both!
The lover feels neglected,
so what's the problem?
The lament of Hafez
is quite engaging.

"My Soul Burns for You"

اي غايب از نظر بخدا مي سپارمت

O you, hidden from sight,
may God keep you.[15]
From your avoidance my soul burns,
yet from my heart I love you.

As long as my grave clothes are not pulled tight
and not buried underground
don't think for a moment
that I will let go of you.

Before sunrise show me your arched eyebrow,
my guide for prayer;[16]
so that I may raise a bouquet of prayers
to decorate your shoulders.

If I must, from Harut of Baghdad,
I will learn
a hundred different spells
to bring you back.[17]

O, neglectful physician,
I will come to you deathly ill
that you may ask about your patient!
I am waiting for you!

Streaming tears from my eyes
I have dammed up and diverted,
to nourish the seed of love
I have planted in your heart.

For that loving dagger glance
I am thankful.
The spilling of my blood
releases me from my grief of love.

I cry, hoping that
this flood of tears
will water the seed of love
I've planted in your heart.

Shower me with your generosity
so that by the burning of my heart,
gems from my eyes,
will be raining at your feet.

Hafez, wine, a beloved and nonchalance[18]
are not your style.
Yet, these you do
and I hold them not against you.
~Ghazal 91

Paraphrase of Ghazal 91:

Feeling abandoned,
longing for reconnection,

feeling the grief of love,
trusting that something positive
will come from tears of grief.

The following poem, artfully inscribed on a plaque, was given to us as a gift of appreciation by a group of North American friends visiting Iran:

"Be Joyful, the Rose Blooms!"
دوستان وقت گل آن به که به عشرت کوشیم

Those knowing the heart's ways, say:
"O friends, at the season of the rose
let's be joyful.
Listen to the heart!"

But no one is happy;
the time for joy is passing.
The remedy is this,
we'll sell the prayer rug
to buy wine!

The time is ripe for joy.
O God send the beloved
with whom we may sip
glowing wine.

This earthly life is a clever thief.
Because of this
Why should we not moan?
Why not cry out?

The rose has withered.
We have not watered it with wine,
it burned from regret and desire.
It lacks wine!

Now we are drinking imaginary wine,
from the tulip's cup
but don't be jealous just because
without wine or musician
we are out of our mind.

O, Hafez, it is indeed astonishing,
but to whom can we say
that we, the nightingales,
in the season of the rose,
must remain silent.
~Ghazal 376

Paraphrase of Ghazal 376:

O friends, now is the time
to listen to the heart.

Yet no one is happy;
the time for joy is passing.
I know, let's forget religious law
and focus on love.

O God, send us the beloved
with whom we may know love.

Yet our daily affairs,
they preoccupy us;
we miss the chance!

Our heart has withered;
burned from regret and desire,
the lack of love.

Now we know a different love,
and we are satisfied.

This is very unusual.
Who can understand
that we, the nightingales,
at the season of the rose
must remain silent.

"Adam's Clay in God's Tavern"
دوش دیدم که ملایک در میخانه زدند

Last night I saw angels
knocking at the tavern door.
They mixed the clay of Adam;
they put in a bowl of God's love.

Then, the angels
and the pure heavenly beings
drank intoxicating wine
with me sitting by the dusty road!

The heavens were unable
to bear the trust of creation,
and it fell to me,
one known to be senseless.[19]

Forgive all those seventy-two
warring sects,[20]
for they did not see the truth
and followed their own fantasies.

Thanks be to God,
for God has forgiven me.
For this, Sufis dance
and drink cups of thanksgiving.

God's love is not
the smiling candle's dancing flame,
but a flashing fire,
consuming clouds of moths.

As long as reed pens
have brushed out words,
no one, like Hafez
can brush back the face veil of thought.
~Ghazal 184

Poems given by other Iranian friends. We became acquainted with an Iranian professor of mathematics who was soft-spoken, full of good humor, and a lover of peace. In reading the following poem with him, we captured the image of the second stanza, the meaning of which had eluded us for many months.

"Roses and Hyacinths"

بتی دارم که گرد گل ز سنبل سایه بان دارد

I have an idol,
a rose cluster ringed by hyacinths.
No other beauty even compares
to this spring-like face.

O Lord, what beauty, a thin cloud
decorating the face of the rising sun.
Give everlasting permanence
to the one with eternal beauty.

When I became a lover, I said,
"I've taken the jewel of union."
I did not know that in this sea
there would be these life-pounding waves.

I am not safe from your eye.
I look this way and that
and from each corner I see an ambush,
of your bow and your arrows.[21]

She shakes her binding chains of curls,
scattering the heart dust of her lovers
and then whispers to the talkative morning breeze,
"Please keep our secret."

Scatter some drink on the ground
and listen to the saint's experience,
for these great ones
have many stories to tell.

O nightingale, watch out
for the trap of the smiling rose!
Although the rose is of great beauty
beauty itself is unreliable.

O leaders of our assembly,
for the sake of God, seek my justice!
The beloved spends time with others
but to me is only harsh.

Since I am bound so tightly,[22]
for God's sake take me quickly,
for delay causes calamity
and suffering for the seeker.

Don't forbid me from seeing
the graceful cypress!
Plant it near the spring of my eye,
a source of clear running water.

If you have hope of union,
from my fear of separation
give me assurance.
For in God's presence there is safety
from those whispering doubts.

What excuse can I give for my fortune?
The sly one who agitates the heart
has killed Hafez with bitterness
but his mouth is filled with sweetness.
~Ghazal 120

Paraphrase of Ghazal 120:

I have a beloved;
beauty surpasses the sunrise.
I became a lover
but did not expect the anguish.
I was wounded by
enticing glances.
I was her captive, but
she tossed my heart to the wind.
Listen, the saints have said
beauty itself is unreliable.

She loves others
more than me.
I am helpless;
O God take me.
The waiting is unbearable

Plant her by the spring of my eye
that I may water her with tears.
I have hope;
save me from doubts.

Hafez has a bitter death,
but love is sweet in his mouth.

One winter day when we were living back in the United States
again, an Iranian friend came to visit us at our home in southern
Indiana. We picked her up at a bus stop, brought her to our home,
settled her in with a cup of tea, and listened to her story. In order
to study engineering in the United States, she and her husband had
to jump many hurdles both in Iran and now in the States. When
she came here, she had left her Hafez books behind and so was
delighted to see those same books on our bookshelf. The meaning of
the following poem had eluded us until this friend came to our home
and elucidated its meaning.

"The Cup of the Universe"

سالها دل طلب جام جم از ما ميكرد

For years, my heart sought
the cup of the universe
from our mental images.
That which itself possessed
it desired from a stranger.

The pearl of the universe[23]
is not out there,
yet my heart seeks it from
lost seekers on the seashore.

Last night I sought help
from the saintly tavern keeper
for he knows
how to solve these riddles.

I saw him, vibrant, laughing,
cup in hand.

In the wine's reflection
were disclosed
hundreds of mysteries.

I said: "When did God give you
this mirror of universal secrets?"
He answered, "On the day
God made the blue heavens."

In all my ups and downs
God was with my yearning heart,
but it did not notice
and from afar called, "O God!"

All the intellect's trickery
are like those who, seeing
the staff and white hand of Moses,
built the golden calf.

Be careful. Remember that friend,[24]
his head strung up on a gallows,
his only crime being
he spoke the secrets openly.

If the Holy Spirit would again
give the command,
others would also
do what Jesus did.

I asked, "What about the chains of curls
dangling from our beloved?"
He said, "They are to restrain
the passionate searching heart of Hafez."[25]
~Ghazal 143

Our Persian language teacher arrived at our home each day by taxi. His head was erect, his black hair glistening, and his brown eyes twinkling. He is a man proud of his people, his prophet, his country; he is a proud Iranian. One day, in the course of learning Persian, we read a story about how, during the Iranian Revolution, the Shah of Iran had hundreds of demonstrating, defenseless, mostly women and children killed. As we read this story together, the twinkle left our teacher's eyes, and he became silent. We both knew the United States and its associates were supporting the Shah at that time.

One day near the end of our study in Iran, this teacher asked us, "Which is your favorite Persian poem?" We weren't sure which of the many poems was our favorite, so we deflected the question. Several days later he asked again. Wondering why he kept asking us this question, we finally answered, "'In the Beginning,' by Hafez." Our teacher's persistent asking became clear the day we concluded our study with him: he and his wife gave us an intricate wood carving of the same poem. A translation follows:

"In the Beginning"

در ازل پرتو حسنت ز تجلی دم زد

In the beginning
your radiant beauty burst.
Love appeared;
fire inflamed all creation.

You appeared and watched.
In the obedience of angels
you saw no love.
In your passion to be loved
you inflamed the human heart.

The intellect came to ignite its lamp
from these flames.
The desire for exclusive love[26]

struck like lightning;[27]
the world was forever changed.[28]

The intellect[29] tiptoed in
to observe the place of secrets;[30]
An unseen hand shoved
the non-intimate away.

The fortune of pleasure
fell to the lot of others.
Our sorrowing heart
knew a longing grief.[31]

The upright soul,
reaching for the dimple of your chin,
becomes ensnared
in your spiraling tresses.[32]

In that joyful letter,
as Hafez wrote of your love,
his pen quieted the longings
of his passionate heart.
~Ghazal 152

We had just driven about five hours to visit our Iranian friend. He welcomed us into his apartment, and we were greeted by the aroma of Persian cooking. This friend is also a husband and a father, and his hair has grayed with forty-eight years of living fully. As he cooked dinner and as we ate together, this friend spoke of his recent experiences in Iran, and after a while he developed a slight cough. This cough brought memories for him of thirty years ago when he was one of a few survivors of a poison gas attack during the Iran-Iraq War. He became reflective: "I have come to realize that at that time I was an Iranian fighting my Iraqi brothers, and not only that, but I was a volunteer and they were coerced into fighting a war of which they wanted no part. After many years I have come to realize that I carry the greater guilt, for I was a volunteer and they were coerced."

This time of painful self-reflection for our friend quickly changed to joy as we began to read a Hafez poem together. We had been puzzled and amazed by the meaning we had gleaned from stanza four, but this learned man, who now teaches comparative religion, assured us that this is indeed the meaning.

"The Light of Dawn"

دوش وقت سحر از غصه نجاتم دادند

Before the light of dawn
I was released from grief,[33]
for in that night of darkness
I was given the water of life.

By the brilliant radiance
of God's essence
I was released
from self-seeking.
I was given wine
from a cup reflecting
divine splendor.

O what a blessed dawn,
O what a happy night,
for on that night of measure[34]
I was given a new script.

And there, when I saw
the brilliance of divine essence,
my face, like a mirror,
reflected God's beauty.

I have reached my
desire and my peace.
Is that so surprising?
I am qualified,
like the poor
receiving alms.

That day a voice from beyond
gave me news of my fortune.
I had been given patience
to endure the strain.

These words dripping
with honey and sugar,
they are a reward of patience,
a lollipop from the divine.

The effort of Hafez,
the breath of the rising dawn,
have released me
from the grief of these times.
~Ghazal 183

One of the first Iranian women we got to know was Heidi. She was
a great help to us in understanding the nuances of Persian poetry. She
is a professor of Persian literature and linguistics, she cooks excellent
Persian food, and she is the best at getting a good deal at the bazaar.
We mourned with her the death of her father, and we celebrated the
Iranian New Year with her and her family. We visited the area of her
childhood in northwestern Iran and took a trip with her family to the
Caspian Sea. She is committed to Muslim-Christian dialogue and
has written several papers related to this topic for North American
groups. She says, "Poetry is the ideal medium for expressing the
truth of our most intimate relationship with God, of loving God, and

of being loved by God." It is this friend who recommended that we acquaint ourselves with the following poem.

Heidi helping Wally read a poem.

"My Beloved Does Not Remember"

سرو چمان من چرا میل چمن نمیکند؟

O why does my graceful cypress
have no desire for the rose garden,
is not companion to the rose,
does not remember the jasmine?

Last night I complained to her dark curls
and she said she was sorry.
But that dusky treasure
would not listen to me!

Since that time, my wandering heart
has gone to her dangling curls
and in that long journey
has lost its desire to return.

I take my stand before her,
pleading to be heard.
She indeed has two ears,
but she does not listen.

On the morning breeze
I can smell your musky perfume,
but it astounds me,
you brought none for me!

Like the morning breeze
breaks off purple petals,
why does my heart not learn
from broken promises?

The heart in seeking her face
has abandoned the soul,
and the soul in desiring her
does not serve the body.

Why is it, when my beloved[35]
offers the dregs of wine,
my body, like a cup,
becomes all mouth?

Don't be harsh with my tears,
for without their help
the Sea of Aden
could not form pearls.

Hafez, did not heed advice,
and was killed by your winking glance.
The sword is fitting
for the one not heeding pain or advice.[36]
~Ghazal 192

I (Wally) had visited an Iranian clinical laboratory where one of my friends was working, and as I waited for him, I sipped a cup of tea in the library area. Suddenly the director of the laboratory appeared. He was about forty-five with some gray in his beard. As he smiled and greeted me, he took off his lab coat, poured me another cup of tea, offered me a cookie, sat down, and opened his book of Hafez poetry (I think that my friend may have told him I enjoy Persian poetry). We talked some about poetry, and then I asked him about his favorite poem, and we read together the following:

"Bewildered by Beauty"
زلف بر باد مده تا ندهی بر باد

Don't send me to the wind
by flipping your hair.
Don't destroy me by sending
those loving glances.

Don't make me drink sorrow
by your drinking wine with others.
Don't send my cry to the heavens
by ignoring me.

Don't make your hair a chain of ringlets
for it would surely bind me.
Don't take my breath away
by dangling your curls.

Don't cause me to abandon self
by being friends with strangers.
Don't cause me grief
by your longing for another.

So that I don't depend on the rose,
let me see your face.
In order that I be free of the cypress,
beside me stand tall.

Don't be the light burning at every gathering,
for if you do, I, myself, will burn.
Don't be in the memory of others
for then you can be in mine.

Don't make me Farhad
by showing the passion of Shirin.
Don't show your beauty openly,
for then I will creep away
into the wilderness.

Be kind to me a beggar.
Listen to my cry
so that my shout will not
reach the door of Asef.[37]

May Hafez not turn away
from your oppression.
For on the day that I became your slave
I became truly free.
~Ghazal 316[38]

One of our Iranian professors was born in the desert town of the
Magi who visited Jesus. To understand the Jewish scripture he had
taught himself Hebrew; to help bring acceptance between Muslims

and Christians he taught himself English. He has a scholar's delicate fingers for holding a pen or a book. On a summer day in June we read out loud an English translation of the Quran while he followed with the Arabic, amplifying our understanding and filling in the background. About a year later he surprised us, saying, "You have learned about the outer aspects of Islam; now you should study the heart of Islam." This Quranic and Islamic scholar then read to us the following poem, which had a dramatic impact on our experience in Iran. When we left Iran, a student friend gave us a plaque of this poem in Persian calligraphy.

"The Veil of Dust"

"The Veil of Dust"
حجاب چهره جان میشود غبار تنم

My mortal dust is the veil
of my soul's face.
How great when this cover
is drawn aside.

This trap is not for me;
I'm a bird of bright melody.
Let me go on to paradise,
for I belong to that meadow.

It's not clear why I've come here
and where I am going;
regretful misery;
I'm so ignorant of my own affairs.

How can I worship
even in this holy space
when I'm stuck together with
naught but sticks and mud?

If a delightful fragrance
comes from my heart of grief,
don't be surprised, for I know the pain
of the desert-stranded musk deer.

I'm the gold stitching of a shirt,
but don't look,
for inside are hidden
a candle's burnings.[39]

O God, come!
Take me from myself.

> With you, no one will hear from me
> the words, "I am."
> ~Ghazal 342

We have a special friend who lived near us. He stands a head taller than most Iranians and has grown a red beard. Although he was born in New York, he has married an Iranian university professor and has learned to enjoy *doogh*, a popular carbonated yogurt drink. He is frequently asked to comment on political events in Iran, to which he responds, "Do you really want an American to make remarks about your own politics?" This always quiets these types of questions, at least for a while. Once when meeting with an advanced Islamic scholar, he began reciting a poem and was quickly joined in the recitation by this learned man. As we left Iran, this poem was given to us beautifully written on a wooden plaque.

"Disaster to Safety"

ما بدین در نه پی حشمت و جاه آمده ایم

> We've not come here
> seeking honor and glory;
> from disaster
> we've come seeking safety.
>
> We're travelers of the household of love;
> we've traveled the whole way
> from before birth
> to here where we live.
>
> From paradise we saw
> your winsome smile[40]
> and we've come seeking
> your life-giving love.

For this treasure,
kept safely by Gabriel,
we've come begging
at the door of the king.

O ship of mercy,
where is your anchor of grace?
We've come to this sea of generosity,
but really we're drowning in sin.

Surely we've lost our respect.
O cloud of mercy, rain on us,
for to God's record of deeds
we bring our black marked page.

Hafez, throw away those
woolen shirts,
for we are coming with burning desire,
following the caravan of love.
~Ghazal 366

Paraphrase of Ghazal 366:

We've not come
seeking recognition.
We've come at your invitation
to love and be love.

But we are sinners
in need of your mercy.

We must discard
our own piety
and come to you
just as we are.

147

It had been a long day, we were tired, and we had one last visit on our schedule. We, together with a Mennonite Central Committee learning tour group, had traveled to the southeastern part of Iran and had been invited to visit a prominent Islamic scholar. We entered the room, already crowded with other visitors, reporters, TV cameras, and bright lights. We were introduced as Mennonites, a group seeking peace. We had some discussion with him on our different understandings of how to work toward peace and justice. As he became convinced that we see peacemaking from the perspective of Jesus's example, he concluded our visit in affirming and encouraging us by quoting the third stanza of this poem of Hafez:

"Planting and Reaping"

مزرع سبز فلک دیدم و داس مه نو

I saw the sky, a planted field
and the sickle of the new moon.
I thought of my own planting
and the time of reckoning.

"O, my destiny! You are sleeping!
The sun is rising!"
She said, "Don't lose hope
over all that's past."

If you, like Jesus,
have a clean face and are naked,[41]
go to the heavens.
From your lamp the sun will receive
one hundred beams of light.

Don't rely on your lucky star;
it's a thief!
It has stolen the crown and belt
of famous kings.

Even though gold and rubies
have dulled your hearing,
the good times are passing;
listen to my advice.

Stay clear of those envious
of your beauty spot.
For in the realm of beauty
neither sun nor moon
compare to your radiance.

O, heavens, don't bargain
for the splendor of love.
For in comparison, your moon
is worth a grain of barley
and two for the Pleiades.

The fire of monkish hypocrisy
will burn the harvest of religion.
Hafez, throw away your woolen shirt
and go!
~Ghazal 407

While living in Iran we had a short vacation from our studies and traveled to the home of an attorney friend who lives near the mountains. The occasion was the celebration of *Eid-e-Ghorban* (Feast of Sacrifice), the event in Abraham's life when, on the mountain, he sacrificed a ram instead of his son. A sheep was purchased and slaughtered, most of the meat given to the poor. Our friend took the remainder to prepare a meal. He turned over a ceramic bowl, used the bottom to whet his knife, cut thin slices, and broiled the meat over glowing charcoal. We shared the meal and then lingered for hours, reading and reciting poetry, and him helping us understand the meanings. He recited the following by Persian poet Rumi (1207–73) and explained the meaning, but it took us another several months

149

to really understand: "Whatever I say, so you can understand, alas, I regret, you understood correctly."

He suggested to us that the ghazals of poet Saadi Shirazi (1210–91) are the best. Later, having heard that I (Wally) was searching for a book of the ghazals of Saadi, our friend Heidi gave me two volumes. I had the opportunity to read and understand this ghazal with an Iranian mathematics professor.

Wally reading a poem with our attorney friend.

"My Friend and My Creator"

وه که گر من باز بینم روی یار خویش را

How great, if I could again
see the face of my friend.
I would, until resurrection,
give thanks to my creator.

The fickle friends ride away
mounted on their steeds[42]
while we walk alone
trailing the caravan.

Creation watches over
very strange people.
Indeed our own friends,
they torment us.

Now I hope that
after soul-searing grief[43]
an ointment may be placed
on my hopeful heart.

The choice is your choice,
do you want war or peace?[44]
We have abandoned
attempts to control.

The person whose feet are stuck
in foreign soil; stay there!
You want to see your homeland?
Only in your dreams!

If you seek happiness,
don't look to other beauties.
And if you do, say good-bye
to sound sleep and peace of mind.

Fire worshipper, Christian and Muslim,
each has a direction for prayer.
For our own prayer
we look toward our beloved.

I seek the dust of her feet,
and again I say, take care!
I myself will not reach up
for the dust on her skirt.

Last night I saw the beauty
secretly speaking to her lover,
"If you seek your own desire
abandon union with me.
But if you seek me
abandon your own control."[45]

Keep your heart's pain covered
let it burn hot.
This is better than showing
your agony to the enemy.

If your grief grows one thousand fold
do not share it with another.
O, friend, take care, for if you speak out
you may not find your comfort.

O, you, royal swaying cypress,
look at me once more,
that I may offer to you
my empty poverty.[46]

My friends say, "Saadi, why
have you given your life to love?
For although you live on earth
you have little to show."

My own contentment
is in my poverty.
Each person knows

what is best for themselves.
~Ghazal of Saadi 13[47]

Just outside the Iranian city where we lived, a cone-shaped mountain of rock and sand rises to a height of about one thousand feet. From its peak we can see the Alborz Mountains of northern Iran. The home of one of our professors, who received his PhD in Montreal, is in these mountains. Living and walking here had helped join his heart with the heart of the divine. He has black hair, intelligent brown eyes, and a calm voice, which became pressured once as he told us of feeling unjustly interrogated by United States immigration personnel when he was traveling as an invitee to attend a theological conference in Philadelphia. He spent many hours sharing with us the inner heart-knowledge of Islam.

One of his favorite poems is "The Garden of the Secret" by Mahmud Shabistari (1288–1340).[48] We read most of this poem with our professor. In this particular poem, the poet is given a question and then responds. Following is a short excerpt from the otherwise long poem:

"Kernel and Shell"

What is the traveler like?
The person who walks the way,
what about this person?
Which person can we say is whole;
who is the complete person?

Again, you have asked, "Who
is this traveler who knows the way?"[49]

The green almond
will be ruined
if, before ripening,
is scraped from its hull.

But when ripe and cured,
outside its hull, it is good.
If you take out the kernel,
you must remove the hull.

Religious law is the hull,
the kernel is the truth.
Between these two
lies the way of nearness to God.

Injury along the way
leads to a defective kernel,
but when ripe and cured,
the shell may be broken.

When the mystic experiences
certain knowledge of God,
like the ripe kernel,
the shell may be broken.

The existence of this knower of God
has no permanent place in this world,
becomes detached,
and never reattaches.[50]

But if the sun warms
the kernel within the shell
there is an attraction
and another cycle begins.

From water and earth
it becomes a tree
with its branches passing
the seventh heaven.[51]

Second time around
more kernels are formed.
One becomes a hundred
by Almighty's will.

First the kernel,
then the tree,
then the kernel.
Like a line from a dot,
and a circle from a line.

The perfect person is like
a round circle
arriving at the end point
which is also the beginning.

After we returned home from Iran, the treasures of Persian poetry and the love of the Iranian people kept surfacing. It was at a tea for persons of various nationalities that I (Wally) sat by an Iranian woman. When the group conversation slowed, she and I began reading Persian poetry. I had in my pocket one of Rumi's quatrains hoping to get some help in our understanding of it. With our heads together, we read, searched the depths of the poem, and shared with others our discovery.

"The Place"

Beyond belief and unbelief
there is a place.
Our passion
is for this place.

The mystic
when reaching this space
lays down their head.
For this place is
neither unbelief
nor belief
nor that imagined place.
It is the place.

CHAPTER 8

Transformation—Seeing with
the Eye of the Heart

The advice of one of our Muslim friends to think of our experience in Iran as a pilgrimage—to experience and encounter God—was wise. Indeed, we encountered and experienced God many times and in many ways during our four years of living in Iran and sharing our lives with the Iranian people.

Mark Nepo, in his work *The Book of Awakening*, writes, "To journey without being changed is to be a nomad. To change without journeying is to be a chameleon. To journey and to be transformed by the journey is to be a pilgrim."[52]

What does it mean "to be transformed"? What transforms into what? And having been transformed, how does one act or think differently? It seems to us that transformation is a lifelong process that, for us, started before we went to Iran, continued while in Iran, and will proceed for years to come. Perhaps transformation is like a journey—a journey toward the transcendent.

"How did living in Iran and relating with the Iranian people enhance *our* journey—our transformation—toward the transcendent?" we ask ourselves.

As we have wrestled with this question, we have come to wonder whether it is not only Iran or the people of Iran who stimulated our transformation in this regard, but we ourselves, as *visitors* or "sojourners" in Iran, who were also responsible for our movement and journey along the path toward the transcendent.

What is it about our identity as "sojourner" or "visitor" in a foreign land that facilitates personal transformation? And, as a visitor and sojourner in another land, do we also or can we also affect the transformation of those with whom we live, relate, and interact?

In her essay "The Aporetic Witness," Susan Biesecker-Mast discusses transformation in terms of truth telling—speaking our truth and witnessing it to others. Biesecker-Mast says that the visitor, at any given time and place, may choose to speak "the truth as we know it." However, she cautions, when we do this, we need to be aware that we also then are speaking a "non-truth," for "the whole truth is simply not ours to tell." "God's full truth always eludes us precisely because it is, as God is, other than us."

The other option, says Biesecker-Mast, is to choose "to not give witness to the truth as we know it but to witness precisely the truth we do not know." At these times, "We must put ourselves on the track of those truths that elude us. We must be relentlessly on the lookout for what we have missed or ignored or hidden."[53] To do this we must listen, and perhaps it is in listening that we experience transformation.

Perhaps it was the Iranian love of poetry that moved us on our journey in Iran, for, like all poetry, it too speaks the language of the heart, where transformation occurs. In our journey toward the transcendent, T. S. Eliot says, "Words strain, crack, and sometimes break under the burden."[54] Perhaps poetry carries this burden more easily.

The Iranians are much more acquainted with mysticism than many Westerners (due in part to their immersion in Persian poetry), and many modern mystics live among them. The well-known Persian poets such as Saadi, Rumi, and Hafez have written many mystical poems about the experience of the transcendent or truth, and almost every Iranian can easily quote their verses.

And perhaps it is the Islam of Iran that also has moved us on our journey and in our transformation. Christians and Jews refer to the divine as God among other names such as Yahweh and *Shaddai.* Muslims call God *Allah* and the Iranians also call God *Khoda, Yazdan,* and *Ezad.* These various names of God are certainly heard more commonly in Iran than in our Indiana hometown. Yet these are verbal symbols of the one who transcends humanity. In Islam God is one: all is a manifestation of God, all creation represents God, yet the total of creation is less than God.

In our pondering about this process of transformation and of being transformed we are helped by stories in which we have witnessed transformation. Following are several of these stories.

On one of my (Evie) return trips to the United States, I was stopped at the US immigration desk and questioned about my reasons for living in Iran. Following many questions about what we were doing in Iran, the officer laid down his pen and papers and asked, "Now, tell me, what is it *really* like to live in Iran?"

I related to him our experience of being welcomed and our freedom to travel throughout Iran without interference.

He listened carefully and then said he was shocked and wondered why Americans seem so attracted to the stories about "terrorists, blood, and guts" rather than welcome, freedom, and hospitality. "I'm glad to hear some good stories for a change," he said. "Welcome back home."

I wondered about the immigration officer's perception of Americans being attracted to stories of violence and terror. During our opportunities to speak about Iran to various audiences throughout the United States, we heard many affirmative comments about our positive, life-giving stories. People seemed eager to engage stories about Iran that transformed their understanding of the Iranian people.

Following a lecture at a college in Kansas, several young people were eager to speak to us personally. Their stereotypes of Iran had been challenged, and they wanted to respond by developing relationships with Iranian young people via the Internet. They wanted names and e-mail addresses so they could begin ongoing relationships to learn more about their Iranian neighbors.

Several of these relationships continued for a number of years. The Iranian youth involved in this letter-writing exchange were delighted to learn more about youth in the United States from a personal relationship. The hearts of these young people were beginning to see each other in new ways.

An American elementary student, Hannah Bumbalough, learning to write in Persian.

In addition to speaking at various college and university campuses, we also shared with several elementary schools. A favorite activity for the students was to learn to write their names and numbers in Persian. After hearing stories about the children in Iran, one teacher asked that each student write a letter to another student in Iran. Thirty letters were collected that began with the words, "Dear friend." These letters were taken to Iran and given to students there. The delight on the faces of the children writing and receiving the letters was remarkable. A simple activity of learning the language of another and of writing a letter to an unknown friend began to open the hearts of these children to one another.

When visiting elementary schools, I (Evie) liked to share some of the stones given to me by the children at the refugee camp in Afghanistan. One time an older elementary student who received one of those stones became tearful when she heard the story about the children living in the refugee camp. She was touched by the gift of the stone and wondered why these displaced children would want to send a gift to their "enemies." "How can I help them?" she asked. I told her the stone could help her remember to pray for the children, for the war to end, and for them to go back to their homes and schools. Later I found out that this student had helped her congregation put together school kits for the Afghan children that could be distributed by Mennonite Central Committee. A small desert stone, given as an act of friendship by an Afghan child, opened the heart of a young American child to find a way to care for a displaced friend.

Young people were especially eager to challenge their understandings of the Iranian people. So was my (Evie) mother. My mother was in her nineties when we made the decision to live in Iran. She was a woman who spoke her mind, and one never had to guess where she stood on any issue, including our decision to live in Iran. My mother did not want us to go to Iran and commented frequently that there is plenty of work to be done here in the United States. She also related many stories she had heard through the media about Muslim terrorists and Iranians who chanted "death to America." Why, she wondered, would we ever choose to go to such a place? Did we want to be killed? No answer from us could ease her anger and fear. So I left for our assignment in Iran with a heavy heart, feeling deeply a call to go yet concerned about the strong feelings of my mother.

After we had lived in Iran for several months, we took a class on Islamic beliefs and practices. During this class our professor talked about the commitment of Muslims to honor and care for their older parents. (It was difficult for many Iranians to understand the concept of placing older folks in nursing homes, as is frequently done in the United States.)

As I listened to these words, I thought of my mother and wondered if perhaps we should have honored her desire for us to remain in the United States. I decided to share my dilemma with our professor and told him about my mother's resistance to our living in Iran and asked how he would have handled the situation if he had been in my shoes. He was silent for what seemed like a long time and then said, "We will pray for your mother." That wasn't what I expected, but I deeply appreciated prayers on her behalf.

Several months later I planned a visit back to the States to visit my mother and family. As I was packing my suitcases, a representative from the institute came to our apartment carrying Iranian tea, pistachios, Iranian candy, and special fabrics. "These are for your mother," he said. I asked him to thank the givers of the gifts and carefully packed them in my suitcase.

I had purchased a small handmade Persian carpet to give my mother, but she would not be expecting gifts from strangers. When I returned home and laid out the various gifts for her, she was amazed and asked me why they were given to her. "They are from our professors and they care about you," I explained. I told her about the care and honor given to older people in Iran, and she liked that! I then was able to slowly tell her stories about our life in Iran.

The next year when I returned home for a visit, once again I was given a variety of gifts to give my mother—saffron, fresh dates, a special box of candy from Esfahan, and dried figs. My mother again received these gifts with surprise and was touched that she was remembered by people who didn't even know her. It was at this visit that she asked if I would be willing to invite some of her older friends over for Iranian tea and tell them some of my stories about life in Iran. We invited five of her friends for tea.

When I was to return to Iran, my mother asked what books about the Prophet Muhammad and Islam would be good for her to read so she could understand "these people" better. I gave her several. She then went into her bedroom and brought out one of her beautiful handmade quilts and asked me to give it to one of the professors who had been sending her gifts. I was shocked. My mother was a remarkable quilt maker, but her quilts were only for her children and grandchildren: they represented an important part of who she was. Even though I had no room left in my already-full suitcase, I packed that quilt and took it to Iran to give to the professor who had been praying for my mother. He received this gift with humility and offered a sentence of thanks to God.

Nearly a year later we had made arrangements to lead a tour group in Iran for two weeks. Before boarding a British Airway jet headed for Tehran, I knew I must call my mother and tell her good-bye. I anticipated some harsh words knowing she was still fearful of my leaving for a country that had received so much negative publicity. I sighed deeply as the phone rang and then I said, "Hello, Mom. I'm in the airport ready to go to Iran and want to say good-bye before I go."

My mom was quiet for a moment and then replied, "Have a safe trip and give my love to the Iranian people."

I hung up, sat down, and pondered her words. She seemed honest in her request to carry her message of love, and I sensed no anger or resentment toward my going.

Three days before we returned home, I got a call that my mother was in the hospital with pneumonia and my siblings felt I should return home. I left Iran immediately but didn't get home in time to say the final good-bye to her. She died as our plane landed in Chicago.

Throughout my growing-up years, I witnessed many yards of fabric and pieces of scraps being transformed into beautiful quilts. In a similar way I experienced the heart of my mother being transformed from fear to love for the Iranian people. This gives me great hope for the future. If the heart of a ninety-seven-year-old woman can see unknown people in new ways, so too can other hearts be transformed.

In addition to my mother, we saw many other North American hearts being transformed via the learning tours to Iran. The experience of visiting Iran always has great impact on the visitor. Stereotypes and misunderstandings are challenged by even a short visit to Iran. One tour group member, after spending two weeks in Iran, wrote, "Along with my suitcase bulging with Iranian arts and crafts, books, beads, and strange food, I am returning home with a heart bursting with even better gifts: new friends, a changed view of Islam and Iran, renewed creative energy, and hope for peace. It was the endless offerings of tea and sweets in the most unexpected places (in palaces, in museums, on rooftops, in meetings); it was the sumptuous meals suddenly spread before us … in (of all places!) a marble factory overlooking a work yard, at the Ayatollah's office, and in a prisoner-of-war camp; it was the countless gifts of food—the universal symbol of community—that shattered negative stereotypes of Iran and of Muslims. We were overwhelmed by the Iranian hospitality and generosity."[55]

One couple who moved to Iran after living a year in an Arab-speaking country commented, "We feel at home here. We think this is the place to begin our family."

Another person, a British professor participating in a seminar on dialogue between faiths, was perplexed by his experience. "Iran, I love it and I hate it!" he remarked. He became aware of the many paradoxes coexisting in Iran.

In these ways and many others, we had the opportunity to witness others' transformations through their engaging and listening to stories about Iran and the Iranian people, through their reading Persian poetry, and through their participation in cross-cultural learning tours to Iran. But how did *we* experience transformation in our own lives?

Some very obvious behaviors were different when we returned

home from Iran. We now always take off our shoes when we enter our home or the homes of others. It seems important as a way to enhance cleanliness and also feels like an act of respect. We have on our calendar important Islamic holidays and make an effort to write to our Iranian friends on those special days. (Incidentally, we always receive greetings from many Iranians on our special holidays as well.) Knowing how important it was for us to be welcomed in Iran, we try to welcome people from other countries who are visiting our country. When we are aware of Iranians visiting the United States, we may travel to meet them and/or offer an invitation for them to visit us in our home. Now we usually begin our prayers acknowledging the divine as merciful and gracious as we read in Psalm 103. Hanging on the walls of our home are Persian poems and handcrafted Persian clocks, constant reminders of the people and country we have come to know and love.

More significantly, a deeper change has occurred within my (Evie) heart. I have gained a deep respect for different faith traditions and have grown in my own faith by listening to how others experience and understand the divine. My personal identity has enlarged to see myself connected and concerned about *all people* of the world. My religion is now *love*, for it is only love that will transform us and our troubled world.

Part of my (Wally) transformation was the experience of mining for jewels among the Persian poems. Someone would refer a poem to me, and becoming acquainted with this poem was like mining for jewels. Each poem has its own unique set of metaphors and designs to present yet another fresh way of describing the lover's relationship with the beloved.

One night, after living in Iran for about one year, I had a dream. In this dream I was looking into a mirror. I was facing the mirror, as if it were from my left side, peeking in. And I saw my reflection; a dark face with fine features, an attractive face and nice to look at. The image/reflection in the mirror was wearing a dark green shirt buttoned up at the neck. (There are four different symbols of an Iranian Muslim man conveyed by this image.) In the dream I was calm, but the next day while reflecting on the dream and its meaning I felt the tension of my identity being stretched.

Sometime later while we were having a conversation with a group of university students, one student who was impressed by my statements of affinity for Islam said, "We hope to interview you again after you have become Muslim." How does one respond to a statement like this in a way that maintains the dialogue and preserves the tension of two different faiths? I responded by saying, "While you are waiting for me to change, I am in the meantime, because of Islam, becoming a better Christian."

As we see with the eye of our heart, there are times and places where we will choose to witness persuasively to the truth as we know it. However, when we stand with the elephant in the dark room, we might do well to "witness the truth that we do not [yet] know."

ENDNOTES

[1] Rumi, *The Mathnawi*, vol. 3, trans. and ed. R. A. Nicholson (Tehran: Booteh, 2002), lines 1257–66. The translation from the Persian, of this segment, is by the author.

[2] Dina Habib Powell, Assistant Secretary of State for Educational and Cultural Affairs, *Building Bridges*, *ejournalUSA*, July 29, 2007.

[3] Permission to publish was granted by Elizabeth Johnson, Iran learning tour member, 2005.

[4] Rumi, *The Mathnawi*, vol. 2, lines 3668–75.

[5] Evelyn Shellenberger and Maria Linder-Hess, *A Common Place* (Akron, PA: Mennonite Central Committee, April 2003), 14. Permission to publish granted.

[6] Thomas Merton, *Conjectures of a Guilty Bystander* (New York: Doubleday, 1996.)

[7] Joan Hawkinson Bohorfoush, *Scarves of Many Colors* (Portland, OR: Joan Hawkinson Bohorfoush Memorial Foundation, 2000), 6.

[8] All the poems in this chapter have been translated from Persian by the authors.

[9] Literally, *rendan* (plural of *rend*).

[10] Hafez Shirazi, *Divan-e ghazaliat Hafez Shirazi,* with commentary by Dr. Khalil Khatib Rahbar (Tehran: Mahtab, 1998).

[11] Literally, "O my moon faced Cannanite (Joseph), you will have a castle in Egypt when …"

[12] Literally, "Act as a rend" (in other words, "Act like you don't care").

[13] Literally, this line is a tribute to Haji Qavam, a court advisor at the time of Hafez.

[14] The tavern is the place where the unrestrained drinking of wine and drunkenness is the symbol of the passionate experience of God's love.

[15] In Shia Islam, this may be the Twelfth Imam; in other religions, a guiding divine presence.

[16] Muslims in Iran, during corporate prayer, face an arched niche, which indicates the direction toward Mecca. Thus the arched eyebrow.

[17] Quran 2:102.

[18] The Persian term is *rendi*, which, as discussed above, carries the meaning of extravagant speech or action without regard to what others might think.

[19] Quran 33:72.

[20] This is referred to in Islamic traditions.

[21] Meaning your eyebrow and your eyelashes.

[22] Literally, "Since I am prey bound to the packhorse."

[23] Literally, "The jewel of the clam shell of the universe."

[24] This refers to Mansur Hallaj, a tenth-century mystic who expressed his nearness to God by saying, "I am Truth."

[25] Here the curls of hair are compared with chains of iron to restrain Hafez from going too near.

[26] This refers to the common theme in Hafez of the tension between knowing through the intellect and experiencing through the heart.

[27] This might mean "divine revelation."

[28] A possible meaning here is, "Put the intellect in its place."

[29] Literally, "the imposter."

[30] In other words, the heart.

[31] This is a common theme: the longing for union with God, which one may see in another's experience but lacking in one's own.

[32] That is, the beauty of God is in itself a barrier to intimacy with God.

[33] The source of this grief is perhaps his sense of separation from God.

[34] The night during the month of Ramadan when the pattern for one's life for the next year is determined.

[35] Literally, "The one with silver legs who brings the wine."

[36] The death of self is fitting for those not fearing pain.

[37] In Islamic tradition he was an advisor to Solomon and a person by the same name may have been a court advisor in the time of Hafez.

[38] This last sentence is a quote from the beginning of one of the Persian poet Saadi's ghazals.

[39] Burnings of God's love.

[40] Literally, "The green [luscious] line on your face" (for example, the soft down of your face; your beauty).

[41] The meaning here is to be free of worldly loyalty.

[42] In other words, "My friend prefers to spend time with others."

[43] Literally, the heat of midday.

[44] The poet is now speaking to the reader.

[45] Other mystics talk of this as seeking God for God's own self rather than for God's gifts to us.

[46] Poverty here has the meaning of the absence of personal desire, which leaves no room for the beloved.

[47] *Divan of the Ghazals of Saadi Shirazi*, with commentary by Dr. Khalil Khatib Rahbar (Tehran: Safi Alishah, 1998).

[48] Shaykh Mahmud Shabastari, *Golshan-e-Raz*, with commentary by Behrouz Servatian (Tehran: International Publisher, 2004), lines 312–364. This poem was written about fifty years after the death of Persian poet Rumi.

[49] The answer goes on and on and includes the following example.

[50] Literally, leaves and does not return.

[51] For example, nearness to God.

[52] Mark Nepo, *The Book of Awakening* (Boston: Conari Press, 2000).

[53] Susan Biesecker-Mast, "The Aporetic Witness," in *Practicing Truth*, ed. David Shenk and Linford Stutzman (Scottdale, PA: Herald Press, 1999), 144.

[54] T. S. Eliot, "Burnt Norton," in *Four Quartets* (Orlando, FL: Harcourt Inc., 1943), line 149.

[55] Permission to publish was granted by Elizabeth Johnson, Iran learning tour member, 2005.